Arts
and Crafts
Rugs for
Craftsman
Interiors

Arts and Crafts Rugs for Craftsman Interiors

The Crab Tree Farm Collection

Linda Parry
and David Cathers

With Diane Boucher,
Ann Lane Hedlund,
and Dru Muskovin

In Association with
Crab Tree Farm

W. W. Norton & Company
New York · London

For information about permission to reproduce selections from this book, write to
Permissions, W. W. Norton & Company, Inc., 500 Fifth Avenue, New York, NY 10110

For information about special discounts for bulk purchases, please contact
W. W. Norton Special Sales at specialsales@wwnorton.com or 800-233-4830

Printed by Engelhardt + Bauer GmbH
Book design: Hal Kugeler Ltd., Chicago
Managing editor: The Coventry Group, LLC, Chicago
Production manager: Leeann Graham

Library of Congress Cataloging-in-Publication Data

Parry, Linda.
   Arts and crafts rugs for craftsman interiors / Linda Parry and David Cathers ;
with Diane Boucher, Ann Lane Hedlund, and Dru Muskovin. -- 1st ed.
      p. cm.
     Includes index.
     ISBN 978-0-393-73320-4 (hardcover)
1. Rugs in interior decoration. 2. Arts and crafts movement. 3. Interior decoration—History—19th century.
4. Interior decoration—History—20th century. 5. Rugs—Private collections—Illinois—Lake Bluff.
6. Crab Tree Farm (Lake Bluff, Ill.) I. Cathers, David M. II. Boucher, Diane. III. Hedlund, Ann Lane, 1952–
IV. Muskovin, Dru. V. Title.
   NK2115.5.R77P37 2009
   746.7—dc22

                                   2009029551

ISBN: 978-0-393-73320-4

W. W. Norton & Company, Inc., 500 Fifth Avenue, New York, NY 10110
www.wwnorton.com
W. W. Norton & Company Ltd., Castle House, 75/76 Wells Street, London W1T 3QT

0 9 8 7 6 5 4 3 2 1

JACKET FRONT
Interior of Crab Tree Cottage at Crab Tree Farm.
See pages 52–53.

JACKET BACK
Group of rolled rugs from the Collection
of Crab Tree Farm.

PAGES 2–3
Interior of the former garage and stables at Crab Tree
Farm with a display of Arts and Crafts rugs and furnish-
ings. Photograph by Craig Dugan, Hedrich-Blessing.

FRONTISPIECE
Scroll drugget. Made in India, 1912/16. See cat. 41.

NOTE
Authorship of catalog entries is indicated by initials
at the end of each entry. DB is Diane Boucher,
DC is David Cathers, ALH is Ann Lane Hedlund,
LP is Linda Parry, and DM is Dru Muskovin.

Contents

"[A rug should] be unobtrusive in design, so that it helps to give a quiet and harmonious background to the furniture of the room, and its coloring should be soft and subdued, repeating the tones that prevail throughout the general decorative scheme."

— The Craftsman, 1910

The English Apartment at Crab Tree Farm with a cast-iron fireplace designed by C. F. A. Voysey and a Hammersmith rug designed by William Morris in 1878/81. See cat. 5. Photo by Peter Frahm—Chicago.

Introduction

Gustav Stickley (1858–1942), one of the most important figures in the American Arts and Crafts movement, began designing his simple, rectilinear Craftsman furniture in 1900, eventually extending his interest to include interior design and publishing a magazine dedicated to Arts and Crafts. The rugs used in his Craftsman interiors are, arguably, the most under-studied of all the decorative arts of the Arts and Crafts movement. This book focuses on the rugs that *The Craftsman* recommended as suitable for Craftsman interiors, and which were sold through Craftsman Workshops' catalogs, shops, and magazine. It also considers other rugs that represent designs by artists who influenced the work and philosophy of Stickley. The origins of these rugs vary: some were designed and made in England, Scotland, and Ireland by Arts and Crafts luminaries William Morris (1834–1896), C. F. A. (Charles Francis Annesley) Voysey (1857–1941), Gavin Morton (1867–1954), and Evelyn Gleeson (1853–1944); drugget rugs, inexpensive reversible rugs made with cotton warps, wool wefts, and synthetic dyes, were imported from India by Stickley; and boldly patterned wool rugs were woven with tapestry techniques by the Navajos of the American Southwest.

No discussion of rugs in a Craftsman Arts and Crafts interior would be complete without the inclusion of Crex and Abnákee rugs, which were manufactured in the United States. Although these two rug types were discussed in articles in *The Craftsman,* examples of them are very scarce. We have located one Crex grass rug and three examples of the work of the Abnákee rug makers for inclusion in this publication. While there are no examples of either type in the Crab Tree Farm Collection, it is important to recognize their role in Stickley's vision of the Craftsman interior.

As the photographs that follow show, the rugs at Crab Tree Farm are displayed in Arts and Crafts settings. The choice of a rug for a particular room reflects, as closely as possible, *The Craftsman*'s directive that the rug "be unobtrusive in design, so that it helps to give a quiet and harmonious background to the furniture of the room, and its coloring should be soft and subdued, repeating the tones that prevail throughout the general decorative scheme."[1]

Crab Tree Farm is the only farm in Illinois located on Lake Michigan. Its founding coincided with the peak of the Arts and Crafts movement in North America in the first half of the first decade of the twentieth century. Originally a commercial dairy operation, it has had three owners in its hundred-year history. Over the last thirty years, the farm buildings have undergone extensive renovations, and they now house collections of English and American Arts and Crafts furniture and decorative arts.

The farm was established in 1905 by Scott Sloan Durand (1869–1949) and his wife Grace Durand (1867–1948). Durand, who was the founder of S. S. Durand and Co., a Chicago sugar brokerage, purchased 250 acres of land on Lake Michigan, just north of the village of Lake Bluff, Illinois. Informed by agricultural training, Grace Durand had founded a burgeoning commercial business, Crab Tree Dairy, on twenty acres in the residential village of Lake Forest. There Durand kept her prize herd of Guernsey cows. Escaped animals and the aroma of farm life were a constant source of irritation to neighbors, so the Durands determined that they must relocate.

In 1910 a fire destroyed the original farm buildings on their new farm, prompting Grace to commission Chicago architect Solon Spencer Beman (1853–1914)—who is perhaps best known for his design of the village of Pullman (1880–84) on Chicago's far-south side—to develop plans for a modern facility for her operation. The result was the remarkable assembly of buildings that survive today as Crab Tree Farm.

Beman, who trained in New York and came to the Chicago area with the promise of work after the city's devastating 1871 fire, created a massive central barn surmounted by a clock tower and flanked by four additional buildings and a pair of silos arranged around a central court and reflecting pool. The style of these somewhat-eclectic buildings has been referred to as California Mission, South African, and Scandinavian.

VOL. XVIII, No. 6   SEPTEMBER, 1910   25 CENTS

THE CRAFTSMAN

THE POWER OF THE SMALL INVESTOR
THE DEMAND OF THE TIMES
A VISIT TO CRAFTSMAN FARMS
THE NEW TYPE OF AMERICAN HOME

FORTY-ONE-WEST-THIRTY-FOURTH-STREET-NEW-YORK

Gustav Stickley and the Arts and Crafts Movement in the United States

David Cathers and Diane Boucher

AT THE BEGINNING of the twentieth century, Stickley was revered not only as an Arts and Crafts furniture maker but also as an advocate for good design and a leading proponent of the American Arts and Crafts movement. "Few men in this country have rendered the service in this direction that Gustav Stickley has," stated a 1904 article in *Carpet and Upholstery Trade Review*. "There are few who would deny him the chief place among Americans . . . in creating a desire among the people . . . to abandon pretense and ostentation, and to embrace the belief that real elegance is in simplicity."[2] While his Arts and Crafts ideas were based on several sources, it was British practitioners—perhaps best personified by the designer, manufacturer, and retailer William Morris; the critic John Ruskin (1819–1900); and the architects C. F. A. Voysey and M. H. Baillie Scott (1865–1945)—who most transformed Stickley's views of art, craft, and labor.

Following Arts and Crafts values and precepts, Stickley's firm, the Craftsman Workshops in Syracuse, New York, produced simple, well-made household furnishings that the new middle classes could afford. Stickley created the Craftsman House, an aesthetic that featured a style of domestic architecture with modern, uncluttered interiors that were conducive

OPPOSITE
Cover of *The Craftsman,* September 1910, showing the front of a Craftsman house. Stickley published his magazine from October 1901 to December 1916.

THIS PAGE
Drawing of the interior of a Craftsman library published in *The Craftsman,* October 1905. The magazine occasionally used color renderings to help the reader understand the quality of a harmonious palette.

to "plain living and high thinking."[3] From 1901 to 1916, he published *The Craftsman* magazine, the most widely read and influential American Arts and Crafts periodical of its day. Through its pages, ideas were disseminated to a broad audience by contributors who took a genuine and serious interest in issues like urban and rural poverty, education, art, and design.

Rugs of the Arts and Crafts Movement

The rugs marketed by Stickley were at once useful and beautiful, and they added subdued color, rugged texture, and understated pattern to Craftsman rooms. They could function as a dramatic foil to the rest of the interior or play a complementary role, their conventionalized forms echoing the clean lines of Stickley's furniture. Rugs also clarified the spatial definition of the open-plan Craftsman interior. In some Craftsman houses, for instance, the living room, dining room, and library constituted a single space with little structural division; large rugs demarcated each functional zone. Most important, rugs created and symbolized coziness, comfort, and simplicity. The visually harmonious Craftsman domestic interior could not have been realized without them.

The craft of rug making also mattered to Stickley. The subject was often treated in his magazine, and hooked, hand-woven, and hand-knotted rugs were much in evidence at the Arts and Crafts exhibition he sponsored in 1903.[4] Rug making was also an expression of the Arts and Crafts movement's socially progressive ideals. It was seen as a revitalized traditional "home-craft" that could provide pleasant employment to a needy, often-rural population of undereducated women.

Of course, rugs also had a commercial value for Stickley's Craftsman Workshops. He sold affordable, well-designed rugs in his three retail stores and through his mail-order catalogs, and he frequently advertised them in *The Craftsman*. Stickley bought his firm's handmade and machine-made rugs from workshops, manufactories, wholesalers, and importers; as was often true of retailers of the era, he did not publicly name his suppliers. Selling to middle-class consumers, he marketed rugs under his Craftsman brand for at least thirteen years, which suggests that this merchandise must have been profitable.

Living room of the Ellis House at Crab Tree Farm with two hand-knotted Donegal rugs and a runner of the same design by Gavin Morton and G. K. Robertson, before 1889. See cats. 24, 25, and 26. The house was built in 1993 from plans drawn by architect Harvey Ellis and published in *The Craftsman*, December 1903.

Rugs Recommended for Use in Craftsman Interiors

The Craftsman magazine recommended a wide variety of rugs for Craftsman interiors: "Luxurious Orientals, bright-colored Navajos . . . scotch wool or rag rugs for the bedrooms, grass or fiber or bullock's wool rugs for sun room or porch — they should be chosen always with the idea of appropriateness for the particular purpose, durability of material and weave, interest of texture and design, beauty of coloring."[5]

Stickley began showing rugs in Craftsman interiors by early 1901, when the firm issued its second Arts and Crafts furniture catalog, *Chips from the Workshops of Gustave [sic] Stickley*. According to the catalog, this furniture was marketed to "the middle class individual," who would find that Stickley's workshop offered "a new world of color." It achieved these rich color effects in several ways: matte finishes emphasized the cabinet wood's natural grain and texture; Grueby tiles in "rich Veronese greens and blues and vivid orange" were set into tabletops; and rush seats, upholstery fabrics, and leather were used to accent pieces. In 1901 Stickley's firm neither made nor sold textiles, but the catalog told prospective customers that its furniture was "admirably suited for use with the soft colors of Oriental rugs."[6]

Stickley's initial use of rugs expressed his decorative vision — simplicity, unity, harmonious color, geometric form — but also revealed some uncertainty over what sorts of rugs best suited his evolving ideas about domestic design. Whatever tentativeness he may have felt was swept aside in 1903, the year Harvey Ellis (1852–1904) joined his firm to design and delineate a succession of assured interiors, which, for the first time, fully integrated Craftsman architecture, furniture, metalwork, textiles, and rugs. In a few instances, Ellis recommended rugs by outside makers; and some of the rugs he drew for the magazine revealed his awareness of the designs of Charles Rennie Mackintosh (1868–1928), Baillie Scott, Voysey, and the Navajo. For the most part, though, his Craftsman rugs were products of his own creative imagination. The spirit of Ellis's ideas disappeared from the magazine after his death, but his sense of "total design" shaped the interiors of all subsequent Craftsman houses.

By 1904 Stickley had chosen the kinds of imported and American-made rugs that his delineators would depict in the interiors of Craftsman houses for nearly the next decade. Machine-woven Scotch rugs, hand-knotted Donegals, and hand-woven Indian druggets made of wool covered living- or

Rendering by Harvey Ellis of a living room of a Craftsman house "as seen from the Reception Hall. . . . The rooms are separated only by posts and partial partitions which serve as a basis for seats, bookcases or plain paneling." Published in *The Craftsman*, October 1905.

Interior of the Music Alcove of the Urban House as drawn by Harvey Ellis. Published in *The Craftsman*, August 1903.

dining-room floors. Flat-weave wool or cotton rag rugs that were hand-woven or produced on a power loom — typically featuring wide, contrasting bands at both ends — were usually placed in secondary rooms. Japanese or American grass rugs were suggested for bedrooms, porches, and summer homes. On rare occasions, the magazine recommended a Navajo rug or a hooked Abnákee rug in specific contexts. With these styles of rugs, Stickley closely followed the trends of his time, although in terms of design and marketing, he was often in the vanguard.

Stickley believed that it was important for the retail prices of Craftsman rugs to remain within reach of the firm's middle-class customers. A short article about rugs in the January 1910 issue of *The Craftsman* declared that they should be offered "at a price that . . . most of us can afford."[7] An advertisement in the October 1909 issue of *The Craftsman* provides a further definition of Craftsman rugs, noting that they should have "simple though artistic design, . . . soft colors,"[8] and the durability to match the firm's furniture. Claiming that few manufacturers or retailers offered such rugs, the advertisement explained that the firm had begun designing and commissioning them in order to meet the demands of its customers. The advertisement does not reveal who made those rugs, nor does it offer the names of any Craftsman designers. Despite statements made in Stickley's rug advertisements and catalogs, evidence suggests that few Craftsman rugs were actually designed by the Craftsman Workshops.[9] Instead, a Craftsman rug was seen as any rug offered in a Craftsman catalog or advertised in *The Craftsman*.

Although Stickley did not manufacture rugs, he did choose them, and his choices completed the "elegant simplicity" of the Craftsman house. Because he was primarily a furniture maker and publisher, his name rarely appears in rug-industry journals, but manufacturers were well aware of him. As an article in *American Carpet and Upholstery Journal* commented in June 1915, "Mr. Stickley has done much to lift standards in all branches of interior decoration and is highly regarded by the trade."[10] In turn, *The Craftsman* featured articles on three hand-loomed rug industries: Donegal Carpets, Ltd., and the Dun Emer Guild in Ireland; and Helen Albee's Abnákee hooked-rug enterprise in New Hampshire.

The Rugs of William Morris

Linda Parry

ALTHOUGH HE NEVER SOLD William Morris's rugs, Stickley, in his introduction to the first issue of *The Craftsman*, unambiguously acknowledged Morris's influence, writing that he aspired "to promote and to extend the principles established by Morris, in both the artistic and socialist sense."[11] A year later, in the October 1902 issue, he reiterated this commitment to Morris, "the great model of the free workman: a man who in life and art represents the principles to which *The Craftsman* and the association of which it is the origin stand fully pledged."[12] To further reinforce the connection between himself and Morris, Stickley, the "Master of the United Crafts," adopted Morris's motto, "Als ik Kan" (If I can), and the symbol of the joiner's compass, which was employed by medieval master craftsmen. He intended this motif, together with his signature and the date, to appear on every object produced by his workshop. Morris himself had adapted his motto from that of the fifteenth-century Flemish artist Jan van Eyck: "Als ich kanne," meaning "As I can" or "As I am able," suggested modesty or self-effacement to Morris.[13]

Morris became a manufacturer of carpets as part of his dream to improve the quality of domestic design and the lives of those involved in manufacture.[14] He was also keen to revive one of the most ancient and venerated crafts. Although hand-knotted carpets had been made in a number of centers in Britain since the sixteenth century, the industry had all but disappeared by 1870. Those that were produced tended to be conventional classical or floral designs and were either commissioned for large houses or shoddily produced for the cheaper end of the market. As a result of the renewed interest in travel, and the fascination with the arts of the

Near and Far East in particular, Oriental carpets and rugs became popular furnishings from the mid-nineteenth century, with London serving as the center of a thriving import trade. Oriental patterns became very popular and a number of carpet manufacturers began to make carpets with traditional patterns adapted for European taste.

In an attempt to produce a more modern form of a traditional technique, in about 1877 Morris began experimenting on a small, upright carpet loom in the attic of his workshops at 26 Queen Square in London. He believed that textiles were

OPPOSITE
Detail of cat. 11.

THIS PAGE
On the cover of the first issue of *The Craftsman* (October 1901) Stickley paid homage to William Morris. Most of the issue is devoted to explaining the underpinnings of Morris's Arts and Crafts philosophy.

important components of the home, providing color and texture, and he was already producing embroidered, printed, and woven furnishings. He now decided to expand his range of production to include floor coverings. He had a clear idea of what he hoped to achieve and was uncompromising in his pursuit of it.

In 1879, with the assistance of a Glasgow carpet weaver, Morris installed full-scale looms in the boathouse of his London home, Kelmscott House, located by the River Thames in Hammersmith. A number of hand-knotted floor coverings were made there, including a range of small rugs intended for use as wall decoration or in suitable domestic settings such as bedrooms (see cats. 5 and 7). From this point on, all Morris carpets were given the epithet Hammersmith, even when production was moved away from the area. Some of these early versions have a hammer sign, and occasionally they also have waves woven in the border (see cat. 5), a trademark that is not seen on later products. Morris studied and collected Oriental rugs, which he used both on the floors and as decoration on the walls of his home, and these became the main inspiration for his work. Although preferring the design and practice of Persian carpets, he was realistic in his own ambitions, adopting a technique using Turkish knots. This did not allow fine detail but suited the broad style of his floral designs. With the 1881 move of the firm's manufacturing base to factory buildings at Merton Abbey in Wimbledon, south of London, he was able to construct much-larger looms, one of which was twenty-five feet wide. This allowed him to produce more ambitious and complex designs. From the late 1880s, Morris's assistant, John Henry Dearle (1860–1932), designed most of the new patterns for rugs made by the firm. Dearle's style resembled, but did not mimic, Morris's, and later rugs produced by the firm, many of which were commissioned for some of the most exciting new homes of the day, maintained a high standard of workmanship and originality in their designs (see cat. 12).

Morris was also responsible for inspiring a renewed interest in machine-woven carpeting in Britain. This cheaper form of furnishing had previously been used only in secondary parts of the home, such as service corridors and bedrooms. Despite his belief that such carpets were "makeshifts for cheapness sake,"[15] Morris produced an original range of designs. He commissioned some of the leading carpet manufacturers to produce the designs, which were sold under his name in his shop on Oxford Street.[16] This included pile carpeting (Wilton and Axminster-type) and flat weaves (Kidderminster or Scotch),[17] both of which were available in a range of colorways, widths, and borders (see cats. 2, 4 and 13).[18] Less than ten different machine-woven carpet designs were put into production, yet their commercial success led to the wider use of this form of floor covering. It also meant that Morris carpeting became available to a number of clients who were unable to afford hand-knotted Hammersmiths.

Morris's rugs were frequently exhibited in London and sold throughout Europe and the United States. His influence over contemporary designers, makers, and interior designers throughout the world emanated not just from his reputation as one of the founders of the British Arts and Crafts movement, but also from his very practical and pragmatic approach to design and production. His work was frequently illustrated in contemporary magazines, and his lectures, in which he set out his hopes and fears for future artistic endeavors, became widely known within artistic communities. Speaking to the Arts and Crafts Society in 1893, he explained his simple but effective design philosophy for rugs: "Never introduce any shading for the purpose of making an object look round. . . . Beautiful and logical form relieved from the ground by well-managed contrast or gradation, and lying flat on the ground will never weary the eye."[19] This idea represented the antithesis of fashionable nineteenth-century carpet design prior to Morris's involvement. As for most Victorians, the goal of employing rugs in interior design had been to create the illusion of depth, space, and volume in order to give visitors the impression of walking through a garden of flowers.

Sample of "Grass" or "Daisy" Machine-Woven Wilton Carpet

Designed by William Morris, 1870/75
Manufactured for Morris & Co. by Yates & Co. and its successor,
Wilton Royal Carpet Company, Wilton, Wiltshire
Carpet made from joined strips of Wilton machine-woven carpeting
in wool, with jute weft
442 × 335.3 cm (174 × 132 in.)

William Morris helped popularize machine-woven carpeting for the home. Before he began promoting it, such carpeting was used sparingly and only in areas of the house that were considered of secondary importance, such as corridors and bedrooms. It was sold in twenty-seven-inch-wide strips that were then seamed together to comprise the full room size and finished with a contrasting border. This carpet is made from five joined widths but no longer has its border. Morris's source of inspiration for the design was a hanging seen in the fifteenth-century illuminated manuscript *The Dance of the Wodehouses*, from *Froissart's Chronicles*; he had studied the manuscript at the British Museum as a young man. Morris continued to use daisy patterns throughout his career. This pattern was also available as three-ply Scotch or Kidderminster and Brussels (uncut pile) carpeting. Altogether Morris & Co. advertised twenty-four different Wilton carpet designs that were initially priced at $.74 per yard. A footstool covered in Grass Brussels carpeting can be seen in the drawing room at Kelmscott Manor in Gloucestershire, Morris's country home, and almost certainly dates from the time that the Morris family lived there. LP

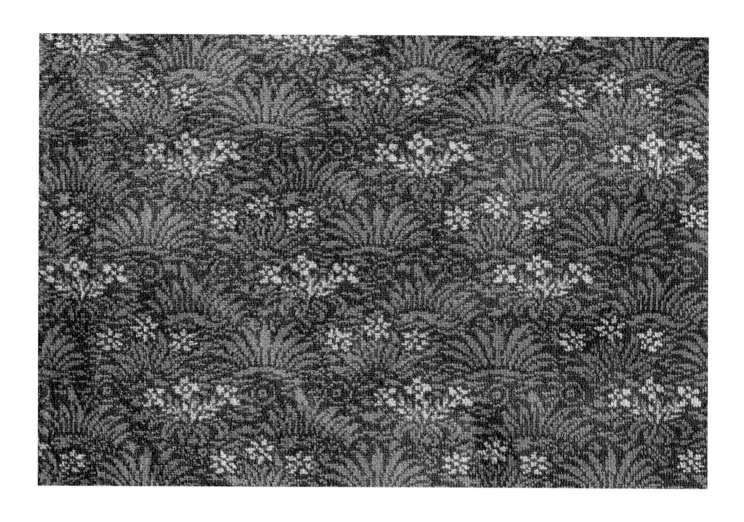

<u>Cat. 2</u>

Sample of "Wreath" Woven Kidderminster (Ingrain) Carpeting

Designed by William Morris, c. 1875
Woven for Morris & Co. by the Heckmondwike
Manufacturing Company, Yorkshire
Machine-woven Kidderminster carpeting in wool, with jute binding wefts
55.9 × 40.6 cm (22 × 16 in.)
PROVENANCE: A country house in southeast England
Haslam & Whiteway, London, 2008

It is assumed that this carpeting is in the "wreath" style, which is referred to but not illustrated in the catalog of the 1899 Arts and Crafts exhibition in London.[20] However, two different Morris patterns for machine carpeting could claim this descriptive name. Stylistically, the pattern dates from about 1875 and is similar to two others registered with the Patents Office on Christmas Eve of that year.

By the mid-1870s, Morris was keen to add floor coverings to the range of domestic goods — furniture, tiles, stained-glass windows, wallpaper, and printed cottons — sold by the firm. Kidderminster (also called Scotch, ingrain, and inlaid) was the first type introduced. It was made for Morris & Co. by the newly incorporated weaving firm of the Heckmondwike Manufacturing Company, whose factory was situated near Bradford in Yorkshire. The firm went on to produce a range of two- and three-ply cloths for Morris & Co. Despite being woven as carpeting, the thicker cloth also proved popular for hangings. A church kneeler covered with this carpeting can be found in Kelmscott Church, where Morris is buried. LP

Cat. 3

Sample of "Tulip and Lily" Kidderminster (Ingrain) Carpeting

Designed by William Morris, c. 1875
Manufactured by the Heckmondwike Manufacturing Company, Yorkshire
Machine-woven three-ply Kidderminster carpeting in wool,
with jute binding wefts
50.8 × 50.8 cm (20 × 20 in.)
PROVENANCE: Haslam & Whiteway, London, 2007

The "Tulip and Lily" style was among Morris's most commercially successful for machine-woven carpeting. A carpet of this design was used on the floor of Morris & Co.'s London shop (now in the Victoria and Albert Museum, London). Morris also used it on the drawing-room floor of his home, Kelmscott House, Hammersmith, laying Oriental rugs and carpets over it. Many of Morris's designs for machine-woven carpets were used for more than one type of carpeting. However, the "Tulip and Lily" design was made exclusively as a Kidderminster, and a matching chevron border was available to finish off floor squares (made from joined lengths) and specially woven stair carpeting. Morris & Co. advertised six different designs for Kidderminsters; these were available in sixteen colorways. LP

Drawing room at Kelmscott House showing "Tulip and Lily" floor covering. Courtesy V & A Images, Victoria and Albert Museum.

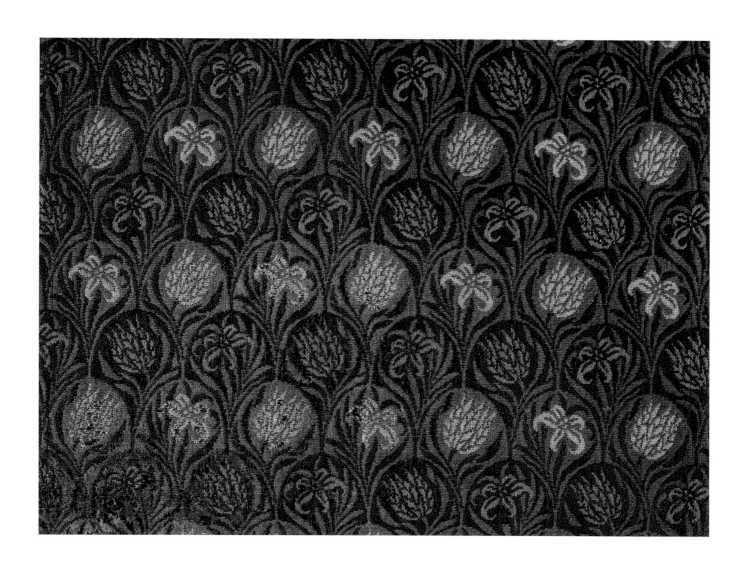

Cat. 4

Sample of "Lily" Machine-Woven Wilton Carpeting

Designed by William Morris, c. 1875
Woven by Yates & Co. and then by its successor, Wilton Royal
Carpet Company, Wilton, Wiltshire
Machine-woven Wilton carpeting, with wool pile and jute wefts
127 × 34.3 cm (50 × 13½ in.)
PROVENANCE: Austins, London
Linda Parry, 2008

It is not known exactly when this design was created, but it was the first produced by Morris for pile carpeting and was mentioned in recommendations for the decoration of the Countess of Charleville's home in Ireland. It became a best seller for the firm. "Wiltons must be classed as the best kind of machine-woven carpets. . . . If well made the material is very durable and by skilful [sic] treatment in the designing, the restrictions as to colour are not noticeable," Morris wrote in the firm's brochure for the Boston Foreign Fair in 1883.[21] It is likely that the lily design was exhibited there.[22] Morris went on to use the traditional dark blue ground color of this style for most of his larger hand-made rugs and carpets. A wide, bordered stair carpet of this design was woven for the main living hall at the home of John Jacob and Frances Glessner in Chicago. LP

Hand-Knotted Rug

Designed by William Morris
Woven in the coach house of Kelmscott House,
Hammersmith, London, 1878/81
Hand-knotted wool (25 knots to the inch) on an undyed cotton warp,
with jute binding wefts
108 × 77.5 cm (42½ × 30½ in.) (without fringe)
PROVENANCE: Esther Fitzgerald, London, 1995
Cora Ginsburg, New York, 1995

This is one of Morris's first handmade carpets. An embroidered panel
of a similar design was also produced by Morris & Co. Inspiration for both
came from a sample of seventeeth-century lacis (darned lace) acquired
by the South Kensington Museum (Victoria and Albert Museum) in 1875.
The maker's mark of an M, waves, and a hammer, which can be seen in
the border, signifies that the rug was woven at Kelmscott House, before
the carpet looms were transferred in 1881 to Merton Abbey in Wimbledon.
From this time forward, all of Morris's hand-knotted carpets and rugs
were known as Hammersmiths, although only a few of the earliest bear
this mark. These small rugs (see also cat. 7) are likely to have been experi-
mental and were possibly made for friends rather than sold commercially.
A few were acquired for the London and Yorkshire homes of George
and Rosalind Howard, who were close friends and clients of Morris; they
were used in the guest bedrooms. LP

Cat. 6

Hand-Knotted Carpet

Designed by William Morris or J. H. Dearle, 1880s
Made at the Merton Abbey Works of Morris & Co., late nineteenth century
Hand-knotted rug (16 knots to the inch) in wool on a cotton warp,
with jute binding wefts
256.5 × 121.9 cm (101 × 48 in.) (without fringe)
PROVENANCE: Collection of Edward Finnes Elton, Ovintgon Park, Gloucestershire
Lord Godfrey Elton, Headington, Oxford
Helena Attlee
Haslam & Whiteway, London, 2008

This unusual rug is meant to be seen from only one point of view. Morris adopted this format from his earliest experiments in hand-knotting in the late 1870s and early 1880s. This example has a hammer mark woven into the border, usually thought to be a sign of early weaving (although this is now impossible to prove). However, the complex coloring — red central ground, blue border, and camel outer border — as well as the unusual design of large, repeating, floral-shaped vignettes, suggests a later date, or possibly that the design was first drawn for another use, such as machine-woven carpeting. The clever inclusion of sprays of willow in the background of the central design and the colorful, lively floral border suggest the work of Morris himself, yet the design appears to have been cut down from a larger one, as the background foliage does not fit the given frame of the field. LP

Cat. 7

Hand-Knotted Rug

Designed by William Morris
Woven in the coach house of Kelmscott House, London, 1879/81
Hand-knotted wool (16 knots to the inch) on an undyed cotton warp,
with jute binding wefts
108 × 86.4 cm (42½ × 34 in.) (without fringe)
PROVENANCE: Private Collection, Edinburgh, Scotland
Esther Fitzgerald, 1989
Cora Ginsburg, New York, 1989

This is another of the small-format rugs produced by Morris & Co. in the
1870s (see also cat. 5); altogether five different designs have been identified.
This example has a pared-down version of the Hammersmith mark, showing
just a hammer. The design uses a traditional artichoke pattern, the source
of which was Turkish and Italian silks of the fifteenth and sixteenth centuries
that Morris studied in the South Kensington Museum. This composition
also includes characteristic Morris floral details such as willow branches and
flower heads. LP

<u>Cat. 8</u>

Hand-Knotted Rug

Designed by the Century Guild, possibly Herbert Horne
Woven by Morris & Co., c. 1884
Hand-knotted wool on a cotton warp, with jute binding wefts
129.5 × 83.8 cm (51 × 33 in.)

Although not designed by Morris, this rug is identical in technique to other early small examples made by Morris & Co. (see cats. 5 and 7). The firm produced rugs for the Century Guild, a commercial organization formed in 1882 by three designers: A. H. Mackmurdo, Selwyn Image, and Herbert Horne (1864–1916). A precursor of the Arts and Crafts Exhibition Society, the Guild survived for only a few years. Significantly, Morris & Co. advertised in *Hobby Horse*, the Century Guild's influential magazine, which was first published in 1884. Of the two existing rug designs thought to have a Morris & Co. and Century Guild provenance, this is, stylistically, the furthest from Morris's other designs. Of the three designers associated with the guild, it is stylistically closest to the work of Horne. LP

"Little Tree" Hand-Knotted Carpet

Designed by William Morris, c. 1880
Woven at the Merton Abbey Works of Morris & Co., 1888
Hand-knotted carpet of wool (28 knots to the inch) on a cotton warp,
with jute binding wefts
233.7 × 108 cm (92 × 42½ in.)
PROVENANCE: Alexander Ionides, 1 Holland Park, London
Keshishian, London, 1992

This design likely dates from the period just before or soon after Morris & Co.'s move to their Merton Abbey Works near Wimbledon in 1881. Described as a "long cheerful room where the carpet looms are built," the new workshop's extra height and roominess allowed the firm to produce many more carpets than before.[23] All of the carpet weavers working for Morris & Co. were young women. The border of the "Little Tree" design became a firm favorite and was used a number of times with other central forms. It was also used for machine-woven carpets with plain fields. Earlier versions of this design were woven with a different border design.

This carpet was commissioned by A. A. (Aleco) Ionides for his house at 1 Holland Park, London, and was one of two carpets proposed for the morning room, which had parquet flooring. This, the smaller of the two, was made for the window alcove. Documentation includes an estimate dated June 18, 1888, which quotes Morris as suggesting "a deep rich red ground broken by foliage and a rich blue border."[24] The coloring of this carpet is reversed from that proposed in the estimate. The final bill of £17 for the rug is dated October 23, 1888. The rug can be seen in one of a set of photographs of the house taken by Bedford Lemere for the family.[25]

A version of "Little Tree" was exhibited at the 1899 Arts and Crafts exhibition.[26] James Morton bought a different version of this rug with his first earnings. There are others in the William Morris Gallery, Walthamstow; and the Museum of Applied Arts, Budapest. LP

An estimate from Morris & Co. to A. A. Ionides. The first page mentions "a good rug for the window" and the overleaf gives the size and price for the "Little Tree." Courtesy V & A Images, Victoria and Albert Museum.

Interior of 1 Holland Park showing in front of the window a version of "Little Tree" commissioned by A. A. Ionides and woven by Morris & Co. Courtesy V & A Images, Victoria and Albert Museum.

"Black Tree" Hand-Knotted Carpet

Designed by William Morris, 1885/87
Made at the Merton Abbey Works of Morris & Co., 1890s
Hand-knotted carpet in wool (28 knots to the inch) on a cotton warp,
with jute binding wefts
231.1 × 153.7 cm (91 × 60½ in.) (without fringe)
PROVENANCE: Peter and Alice Jones, London
Philips, London, October 10, 2000
H. Blairman & Sons, London

The use of large, traditional medallions in one-way directional designs increased as Morris's fascination with early Oriental carpets deepened. First used about 1885, this style followed a group of two-way patterns that included "Little Tree." When acquired from a London auction house in 2000, this carpet was believed to have been originally purchased in the 1890s from the Oxford Street shop of Morris & Co. by Peter and Alice Jones for their house in St. Peterburgh Place, Bayswater, London. A rug of this design was exhibited at the 1889 Arts and Crafts exhibition, London.[27]

Hand-Knotted Carpet, Possibly "Flowery Field"

Designed by William Morris, c. 1885
Made at the Merton Abbey Works of Morris & Co.
Hand-knotted carpet in wool (25 knots to the inch) on a cotton warp,
with jute binding wefts
241.3 × 157.5 cm (95 × 62 in.) (without fringe)
PROVENANCE: Keshishian, London, 1997

Because few of Morris's later rugs conform to the designs of his larger carpets, it is difficult to date this example. From about 1885, however, Morris was absorbed with designing and weaving tapestry panels, all of which have millefleur grounds showing dispersed clumps of British garden flowers similar to those on this rug. The design is probably that known as "Flowery Field." It fits the size and description given by C. C. E. Tattersall in *A History of British Carpets* — "upright flowering plants on a green field: yellow border with wavy leafy stems."[28]

Three versions of this rug are known. In 2000 John H. Bryan III purchased a version in green and olive, and a third version has a dark blue ground and red border and was specially commissioned from Morris & Co. around 1895 by the Barr-Smith family of Adelaide, Australia. It was sold at Sotheby's, Melbourne, in 1993.

This rug may be that displayed at the London Arts and Crafts exhibition in 1889, which was described as "Designed by William Morris.[29] Made by the Misses E. and M. Merritt, L. and M. Phipps, C. Adaway and D. Penn."[30] It was exhibited again in 1899. A scaled watercolor rendition of this rug and others was produced in the studio of Morris & Co. and shown to prospective customers. Inscribed "5.0 × 8.0" and "£20.10.0. (£20.50p)," it was sent to the Victoria and Albert Museum in the 1920s, where it was photographed before being returned to the shop. LP

Scaled watercolor design for "Flowery Field." Courtesy V & A Images, Victoria and Albert Museum.

Hand-Knotted Rug

Designed by J. H. Dearle, c. 1890
Woven at the Merton Abbey Works of Morris & Co., 1890–95
Hand-knotted wool (30 knots to the inch) on cotton warp,
with cotton binding wefts
204.5 × 114.3 cm (80½ × 45 in.) (without fringe)
PROVENANCE: Clare and Robert Franses, London, 2006

From 1890 Dearle drew all of the new designs for woven and printed textiles
and carpets at Morris & Co. On Morris's death in 1896, Dearle became artistic
director of the firm. The design of this rug is unusual, as it has a central
field of only two colors. Dearle also produced a range of striated rugs and
carpets with patterned borders and plain centers, which were popular in
the 1890s and early twentieth century. Early border patterns were frequently
repeated with different centers, and customers could select both elements
when ordering a rug. The border of this rug is the same as that of the "Little
Tree" rug (see cat. 9), which is a conventional red and indigo blue. Here
it is shown in an unusual combination of pastel colors characteristic of the
latter years of the nineteenth century.

A version of this rug was owned by May Morris; she loaned it to
the Victoria and Albert Museum for the 1934 centenary exhibition
devoted to her father. It is now at Kelmscott Manor, the Morris family's
Gloucestershire home. LP

Cat. 13

Runner of Machine-Woven Axminster Carpeting

Almost certainly woven for Morris & Co.
by the Wilton Royal Carpet Company of Wilton, Wiltshire, 1905/10
Patent Axminster power-loom woven rug of wool,
with jute binding wefts and backing
213.4 × 67.3 cm (84 × 26½ in.)
PROVENANCE: Birtles Hall, Cheshire
Paul Reeves, London, 1994

Morris & Co. recommended this type of carpeting for church use, and similar rugs appear in the firm's twentieth-century catalogs as recommendations for carpeting, seating, and kneelers. The published price for carpeting was "in plain or mixed colourings, 27 in. wide from 8s [shillings] 6d [pence] per yard" with borders at "4s 6d, 5s 9d and 7s 8d per yard." Wilton produced a wide range of power-loom "Patent-Axminster" carpets for the Morris firm. These were woven with an already patterned chenille weft (itself woven in a preliminary technique). The chenille formed the pattern and appeared only on the surface of the carpet; it was then loosely woven onto a coarse backing that, in Morris's carpets, is always visible as a plain black cloth on the reverse. Because this technique allowed a much bolder pattern than machine-woven types, the firm recommended it as a cheaper alternative to a Hammersmith rug. These carpets were also thicker than their machine-woven counterparts and proved popular as runners and stair carpets. LP

Cat. 14

Sample of Wilton Carpeting

Probably designed by J. H. Dearle, 1905/10
Manufactured for Morris & Co.
by the Royal Wilton Carpet Company, Wilton, Wiltshire
Joined narrow strips of Wilton pile carpeting in wool, with jute binding wefts
177.8 × 88.9 cm (70 × 35 in.)
PROVENANCE: Birtles Hall, Cheshire
Paul Reeves, London, 1994

Although this is an unrecorded design characteristic of Dearle's work, the border was used a number of times (see cat. 13) and is one of a range that was commercially available from Morris & Co. In the late 1880s, Dearle took over from Morris as the main pattern designer for Morris & Co., although there is evidence that Morris kept a close eye on the firm until around his death in 1896. In 1905 Morris & Co. was restructured, with the management controlled by a board of directors and Dearle in charge of all designs and production. At this time, a new range of goods was produced to recapture a flagging market. LP

The Rugs of C. F. A. Voysey

Linda Parry

"IN THE COURSE OF HIS TRAVELS [to France and England during the winter of 1902–03] seeking for whatever was inherently good," stated the June 1912 issue of *The Craftsman*, "Mr. Stickley had the opportunity in England of talking over the arts and crafts problem at length with Mr. Charles F. A. Voysey, and when he returned to America he brought home specimens of this craftsman's work, which at the time was regarded as the most significant and individual in England."[31]

C. F. A. Voysey, together with M. H. Baillie Scott and Charles Rennie Mackintosh, was among the most talented members of the second generation of British Arts and Crafts architects and designers. All had a decisive influence on the movement in the 1890s and early 1900s, creating houses with new design ideas and participating in the production of various types of decorative arts.

In 1882 Voysey set up his own architectural practice, supplementing his income by designing textiles, wallpaper, furniture, and other decorative objects. By the time Stickley met Voysey, the latter was enjoying a reputation as one of the leading figures in British architecture and design.[32] From the late 1880s until the mid-1930s, Voysey drew an enormous number of repeating designs for wallpapers, printed and woven textiles, and carpets and rugs. He sold these to many different British wallpaper, textile, and carpet manufacturers, including the Kidderminster firm of Tomkinson and Adam and Templeton's of Glasgow, both of which produced machine-woven carpets. However, his most enthusiastic client was Alexander Morton (1844–1921), a Scottish maker of woven furnishings and both machine-made and hand-knotted carpets. Voysey was a shrewd businessman and worked under

contract to both Morton and Tomkinson, providing a number of designs each year for which he received a specific fee. This did not mean that he could not also sell designs to other companies, but it did guarantee him an annual income.

Voysey never wasted a design. He continually updated them and would frequently sell the same pattern to be used for a number of different techniques. Originally conceived as a wallpaper, the design of the Duleek rug (see cat. 15) was also produced as a woven woolen furnishing fabric and

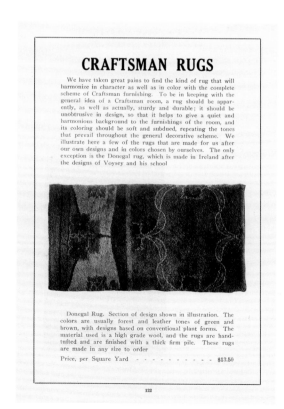

OPPOSITE
Detail of cat. 19.

LEFT
Page from *Craftsman Furniture Made by Gustav Stickley at the Craftsman Workshops,* 1910, offering Donegal Voysey-inspired rugs at $13.50 per square yard.

window gauze. Similarly, another rug attributed to Voysey (see cat. 23) was also used for the wallpaper "Paon."

We know nothing more about Stickley's meeting with Voysey, but we do know that Stickley visited the Arts and Crafts Exhibition Society's seventh exhibition at the New Gallery, London, in January 1903, where Voysey was an exhibitor.[33] Voysey's display included a hand-knotted carpet produced by the Austrian manufacturer J. Ginkey, which was exhibited by Liberty's and probably sold through its store; a carpet design; and a group of woven textiles designed by Voysey and made by Morton at the Darvel factory in Scotland.

The Arts and Crafts Exhibition Society's first exhibition was held in 1888; Walter Crane, writing in the preface to the accompanying catalog, succinctly laid out its aims: "The decorative artist and the handicraftsman have hitherto had very little opportunity of displaying their work to the public eye, or rather of appealing to it on strictly artistic grounds in the same sense as the pictorial artist. It is with the object of giving some visible expression to these views that the present exhibition has been organized."[34] The society's many exhibitions were extremely influential, and they represented the best in British Arts and Crafts design and craftsmanship. Stickley, looking for ideas for his new enterprise, had carefully timed his trip to London to coincide with the 1903 exhibition. At this time, Voysey's work was at its most original; incorporating birds, animals, hearts, flowers, and trees (usually depicted in silhouette) in tonal pastel colors, his designs have a freshness and exuberance not seen before in British carpets.

The "River Mat" (see p. 55) design, for example, was woven as a hand-knotted carpet by Yates & Co. (later Wilton Royal Carpet Company), Wilton, Wiltshire, one of the few establishments that continued to produce hand-knotted rugs into the middle of the twentieth century. The rug is identical to its rather-unconventional design. This suggests different production methods than those used by Alexander Morton & Co. Because the rugs and design remained in the Voysey family, it is likely

OPPOSITE
Living room of the Crab Tree Cottage at Crab Tree Farm, featuring a hand-knotted Donegal rug designed by C. F. A. Voysey or the Silver Studio, c. 1895. See cat. 23.

that Voysey commissioned the company to make two rugs for him. An American collector purchased one from Voysey's son in 1989. The other belonged to John Brandon-Jones, a member of Voysey's architectural practice, who acquired it following the designer's death; it remains with his family.

A rug of this design was exhibited at the London Arts and Crafts Exhibition Society's exhibition of 1903, where it was described as a hearthrug.[35] The piece received mixed comments, ranging from a description of it as "a quaint panoramic design" to one calling it "a kind of Chinese landscape."[36] The rug was also shown at the Victorian and Edwardian Decorative Arts exhibition at the Victoria and Albert Museum in 1952.[37] A point paper for the carpet has survived in the Victoria and Albert Museum.

Voysey had little technical expertise but was fortunate to collaborate with various manufacturers who interpreted his patterns skillfully. Alexander Morton & Co. was particularly adept at reproducing Voysey's subtle colors with the use of new artificial dyestuffs developed by the firm.

As an architect and advocate of Arts and Crafts principles, Voysey contributed greatly to the precept of the unity of design. He put as much emphasis on the furnishings of his houses as he did on their exteriors, creating room settings that had a close stylistic relationship to the outside of the home. For Stickley, Voysey's interiors perfectly epitomized the new family-oriented design aesthetic: "Preeminently modern in spirit, so that his furnishings achieve harmony in the new English country houses for which they are designed. . . . He plans his furniture for sitting rooms instead of great halls, for libraries where the young folks gather . . . the result is intimate rather than pompous."[38]

Voysey's "River Mat,"
a hand-knotted carpet
measuring approxi-
mately 238.8 × 121.9 cm
(94 × 48 in.), was made
by Yates & Co. Collection
of the John Brandon-
Jones family.

OVERLEAF
Inglenook of the Ellis
House at Crab Tree
Farm featuring Stickley
furniture and a C. F. A.
Voysey–designed
"Duleek" Donegal rug
(1903–07). See cat. 15.

Sample of woven wool furnishing fabric manufactured by Alexander Morton & Co. This weave was sturdy enough to be used for upholstery fabric and can be seen on armchairs of period photos. Crab Tree Farm Collection.

Cat. 15

The "Duleek" Hand-Knotted Carpet

Designed by C. F. A. Voysey, 1897
With a border by Gavin Morton
Hand-knotted for Liberty & Co. in Donegal, Ireland, 1903–07
Hand-knotted in wool (16 knots to the inch) on a woolen warp
345.4 × 279.4 cm (136 × 110 in.)
PROVENANCE: Private collection, London
S. Franses, London, 1988

This popular Voysey design was first produced as wallpaper by Essex & Co. in 1896, and then, soon afterward, as a woven textile (see illustration at left for a sample of the woven textile) and a madras muslin by Alexander Morton & Co. for Liberty's. Finally, it was used as a Donegal hand-knotted carpet; it was first exhibited in this form in the 1903 Liberty's exhibition at the Grafton Galleries, where it was recommended for "dining rooms, libraries and halls."[39] It also proved popular for use in the nurseries of large houses. One example was purchased for a house in Ireland and can now be seen in the nursery of Berrington Hall, a National Trust house near Leominster, Herefordshire. A carpet with this border and a plain red center was sold at Christie's, New York, in September 1992.

It was illustrated in *The Studio* as a wallpaper frieze,[40] wallpaper,[41] and a woven textile.[42] A woven hanging of this design was exhibited in the centenary exhibition *Liberty 1875–1975* at the Victoria and Albert Museum, London. LP

Five Versions of the "Donemana" Carpet

Designed by C. F. A. Voysey, c. 1898
Adapted for carpet by Gavin Morton, who designed a matching border
Hand-knotted by Alexander Morton & Co. for Liberty & Co.
in Donegal, Ireland, 1901/08
Hand-knotted on a woolen warp
Cats. 16–19 are woven at 16 knots to the inch, cat. 20 at 22 knots to the inch

Cat. 16
116.8 × 94 cm (46 × 37 in.)
PROVENANCE: Keshishian, London, 2004

Cat. 17
116.8 × 94 cm (46 × 37 in.)
PROVENANCE: Keshishian, London, 2004

Cat. 18
246.4 × 132.1 cm (97 × 52 in.)
PROVENANCE: Keshishian, London, 2003

Cat. 19
350.5 × 279.4 cm (138 × 110 in.)
PROVENANCE: Kesheshian, London, 1991

Cat. 20
472.4 × 152.4 cm (186 × 60 in.)
PROVENANCE: Sotheby's, New York, December 13, 2007
Tim Gleason, 2008

A sample of a woven textile of this design is in the collection of the Decorative Art Museum in Copenhagen, Denmark. It was purchased from Liberty's in the late 1890s. The "Donemana" proved to be the most popular of all Donegal rugs and, like a number of other Donegal carpets, was named after a small village in Ireland. Many examples have survived, including these five versions. They show how successfully the repeating motifs transferred to a wide range of sizes and formats: from a large carpet (cat. 19), to a short carpet (cat. 18), longer runner (cat. 20), and side or hearth rugs (cats. 16 and 17). The "Donemana" carpet was exhibited by Liberty's at the Grafton Gallery exhibition in 1903. The catalog entry clearly titled it the "Donemana" design, whereas a number of recent published sources refer to it as the "Donemara." The catalog went on to describe it as "a pleasing rendering of tulips and half blown roses," citing "the buds of tulips, on a plain ground, [that] are introduced as a border pattern."[43] This original border can be seen in cats. 19 and 20; the other borders show two simple variations. Writing in the *Art Journal* in 1908, the well-known Scottish carpet designer and journalist Alexander Millar described the "Donemana" carpet as "possessing Voysey's well-known originality and breadth of treatment, which is especially adapted for the coarse fabric."[44] LP

Cat. 16

Cat. 17

Cat. 18

Cat. 19

Cat. 20

Cat. 21

"The Rose" Hand-Knotted Donegal Carpet

Designed by C. F. A. Voysey, c. 1897
Adapted for carpet by Gavin Morton
Woven by Alexander Morton & Co. for Liberty & Co.
in Donegal, Ireland, c. 1899
Hand-knotted wool (16 knots to the inch) on a woolen warp
419.1 × 284.5 cm (165 × 112 in.)
PROVENANCE: Keshishian, London, 2001

BELOW
Detail of the border of "The Rose," a Donegal Carpet adapted by Gavin Morton from a design by C. F. A. Voysey, and woven for Alexander Morton & Co. in Donegal, Ireland, 1898/1909. Hand-knotted wool (16 knots to the inch) on a woolen warp; 365.8 × 365.8 cm (144 × 144 in.). Crab Tree Farm Collection. PROVENANCE: Paul Reeves, London.

Cross-stitched into the back of this version of "The Rose" are the words "DONEGAL HAND-MADE." James Morton described taking designs to Maple's, one of the largest London suppliers of furnishings for the home, which then asked to see actual weavings. The strong coloring of this example is an indication that it may be an early sample made to show Maple's. The more subtle toning colors of carpets woven a year or two later show the influence of Liberty & Co., which had become a major client of Alexander Morton & Co. LP

The Donegal carpet industry was originally established in 1898 in a hayloft in Killybegs (and moved to a factory there in 1901), with subsidiary manufactories set up in Kilcar (1899) and then in Annagry and Crolly (1904). Killybegs remained the main site from which all finishing, distribution, and transport for Donegal textiles was organized.

This Voysey design was initially produced as a silk and wool double cloth from Morton's Helena range. It appears to be the earliest dateable carpet woven in Donegal associated with Voysey. James Morton noted that the seventh carpet woven in Ireland was adapted by Gavin Morton from a Voysey Helena textile of 1897. He further claimed that the carpet "filled a certain want in the trade and [is] to be seen as often as any on the looms to this day."[45]

A carpet with this design was exhibited in 1899 at the Arts and Crafts Society of Ireland in Dublin and was praised by the potter Harold Rathbone in the third *Journal and Proceedings* of the society (1901). It was also shown in the London Arts and Crafts Exhibition Society display of the same year, where it was listed in the catalog as a "Rose Group carpet . . . designed by G. Morton."[46] This could refer to the small trial weaving illustrated in both the *Art Journal* and *Der Moderne Stil*, a leading artistic German magazine, in 1900. The carpet was also shown in the 1903 Liberty's exhibition at the Grafton Gallery. A review in the *Furniture Record* described it as an "Old English design, introducing the Tudor rose."[47] It also mentioned that a large Donegal, possibly this example, took about six weeks to weave.

Like many other designs, "The Rose" could be ordered in any size and a range of colors. A version in pale blues and greens was used in the drawing room of Pentower, Fishguard, Wales.[48] LP

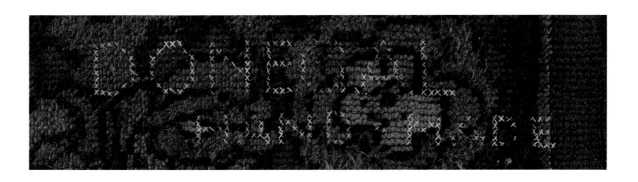

Hand-Knotted Donegal Carpet with the "Lisburn" Border

Border designed by Gavin Morton after C. F. A. Voysey, c. 1902
Woven by Alexander Morton & Co. in Donegal, Ireland, 1905/10
Hand-knotted wool (16 knots to the inch)
264.2 × 137.2 cm (104 × 54 in.)
PROVENANCE: Paul Reeves, London, 1989

The patterned border of this carpet was first used with the "Lisburn" carpet, which had a central floral and trellis design.[49] This version was exhibited at the Grafton Gallery in 1903 and 1907, when it was illustrated in the catalog *Carpets Produced on British Looms*. The original carpet shows a livelier rendition of the border of trailing vines and grapes and is closer in style to Voysey's work. This later example was made around 1905, when a fashion for less complex and fussy designs encouraged the popularity of carpets with plain centers. Also missing from this example are the traditional inner and outer guard stripes (or subsidiary borders) of the original design. LP

Hand-Knotted Donegal Carpet

Designed by C. F. A. Voysey or the Silver Studio, c. 1895
Adapted for use as a carpet by Gavin Morton
Woven by Alexander Morton & Co. in Donegal, Ireland, 1899–1904
Hand-knotted wool (16 knots to the inch) on a wool warp
312.4 × 190.5 cm (123 × 75 in.)
PROVENANCE: Keshishian, London, 1991

This pattern was first used as a printed wallpaper called the "Paon Design" (*paon* is French for peacock). Because no documentation for the rug is known, a positive identification of the designer has not been possible, although it is assumed that it is by Voysey. However, the Silver Studio also produced a number of designs between 1880 and 1910 based on peacocks, and the scale and intricacy of this pattern is similar to designs made there. Further confusion is caused by the fact that the Studio worked in the style of a number of contemporary designers, including Voysey. Incomplete records of Silver Studio sales have survived, and these indicate that the Mortons were good clients. Unfortunately, this design cannot be found among those commissioned from Silver Studio.

The detailed center of this rug is very close to the original wallpaper and shows a high level of technical skill in the weaving. Another version of the rug is part of the Anderson Collection in the Sainsbury Centre for Visual Arts at the University of East Anglia, Norwich. LP

"Paon Design" printed wallpaper. Manufacturer unknown. Crab Tree Farm Collection.

Donegal Rugs of Ireland

Linda Parry

DURING STICKLEY'S FIFTEEN YEARS as the owner and editor-in-chief of *The Craftsman*, he explored a wide range of cultural, political, and economic issues. Given his own childhood, spent in rural poverty on a small farm in Osceola, Wisconsin, Stickley had no illusions about the impoverished state of the countryside at the beginning of the twentieth century. Consequently, one of his main preoccupations in *The Craftsman* was the revival of traditional handcrafts as a means of creating employment in rural areas. His ideas were based on the Arts and Crafts theory that the evils of modern life were directly related to industrialization and city living. In a 1908 editorial, Stickley wrote that when people left the countryside they lost their independence and self-reliance; he explained, "Huddled together in cities it is inevitable that they should come in time to see everything from an artificial point of view."[50] The Arts and Crafts ideal was a utopian, preindustrial way of life, in which people enjoyed good health and pleasant working conditions in a bucolic setting.

The Craftsman, however, recognized that in order for rural industry to make a significant impact on a local economy, it needed to be organized on a large scale and would thus inevitably involve government expenditure. Stickley posited ideas to regenerate rural areas in the United States, such as the introduction of government-funded craft schools. He also cited government-backed ventures overseas as models for the United States. One of these was the Donegal rug industry in County Donegal, Ireland, which manufactured hand-knotted wool rugs.[51]

Alexander Morton's career as a manufacturer began in 1867 with the revival of an ailing local industry in Darvel, near Kilmarnock, in southern

Scotland. Hand- and machine-embroidered gauzes had been an important Scottish industry since the eighteenth century, and within a few years, Morton recruited enough local workers to warrant setting up a factory for the production of machine-made lace. The weaving of wool furnishings and three-ply (Kidderminster) carpeting followed, and by the mid-1890s, the firm was producing a range of fashionable furnishings for a wide international market. Morton sold his wares through Liberty's and other leading London stores, and in turn Liberty's commissioned textiles and carpets from the firm. From the 1880s, James Morton, Alexander's son, was in charge of the artistic direction of the company, and it is due to his careful selection of designs from

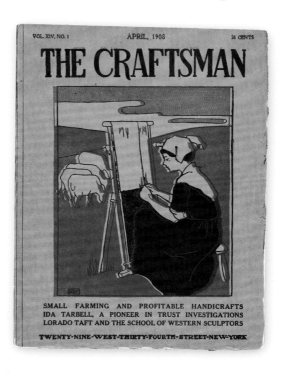

VOL. XIV, NO. 1   APRIL, 1908   25 CENTS

THE CRAFTSMAN

SMALL FARMING AND PROFITABLE HANDICRAFTS
IDA TARBELL, A PIONEER IN TRUST INVESTIGATIONS
LORADO TAFT AND THE SCHOOL OF WESTERN SCULPTORS

TWENTY-NINE-WEST-THIRTY-FOURTH-STREET-NEW-YORK

As if to reinforce one of the tenets of the Arts and Crafts movement, the cover of the April 1908 issue of *The Craftsman* depicts a woman weaving in the countryside.

many of the leading British freelance designers of the day (including Voysey) that the company flourished. Carpets soon became an important aspect of the company's production and, by the mid-1890s, accounted for a quarter of all sales.[52]

In 1895 the firm was reorganized under Alexander's two sons, James and Guy, with Gavin, a nephew, running the design studio. (Gavin was responsible for many of the new designs issued by the firm and for adapting the work of others.) A year later, on the advice of Alexander, James and Guy visited Ireland with the idea of setting up a carpet workshop in County Donegal. Alexander himself became involved in the project and eventually took up residence in Ireland. The venture had a strong philanthropic purpose, as the area was poor and offered little means of employment for residents. However, the Mortons' motivations were not completely altruistic in establishing their first factory in Killybegs, for this project was partially funded by the Congested District Board, an organization created for the purpose of poverty relief. By 1898, 150 girls were employed in a rapidly expanding industry, and subsequent factories were established in Kilcar (1899) and Annagry and Crolly (1904).

The hand-knotted carpets and rugs produced in these factories became known as Donegals. They were made entirely of wool (rugs usually have a cotton or hemp warp), from sheep reared locally, and the industry provided work not only for carpet knotters but also for local farmers, spinners, and dyers. Adopting Morris's chosen technique, the Mortons chose to use Turkish knots in the manufacture of their carpets. Because of the softness of the wool and the depth of the pile, the carpets had a thick, luxurious texture. Designs varied from Oriental themes by G. K. Robertson (cats. 24 and 25), which were given a new lease on life with enlarged motifs and pale coloring, to highly original floral designs by Voysey (cats. 16–20) and Gavin Morton (cat. 32). The colors of these carpets were unlike anything seen before. Most had a green warp, which gave a vibrant quality to the designs when combined with strong reds, oranges, pinks, greens, and purples.

In the conclusion to his report on the Arts and Crafts Society of Ireland's second exhibition, in 1899, the art potter and critic Harold Rathbone (1858–1929) gave special praise to the Donegal carpet industry, noting that it "should prove a source of great wealth to the west of Ireland if the American and other markets be duly fostered."[53] Unbeknownst to Rathbone, Donegal rugs were already being introduced to the United States. James Morton, during a visit to New York that year, had shown Donegal samples to his biggest customer, "who received them with enthusiasm."[54] On May 1, 1899, Hunter and Witcombe, Alexander Morton & Co.'s agents, announced in the *Carpet and Upholstery Trade Review* that they were the sole United States agents for Donegal carpets.[55]

Only a few Donegal carpets can be positively identified as the work of Voysey, although many show characteristics of his style. The reason for this is difficult to determine. There were strong links between Voysey, Alexander Morton, and Liberty's, the London shop that commissioned Donegal carpets. From 1897 Voysey was under contract to the Morton firm to supply a minimum of ten designs for furnishing textiles per year for five years, renewable after this period. These were for furnishing textiles.

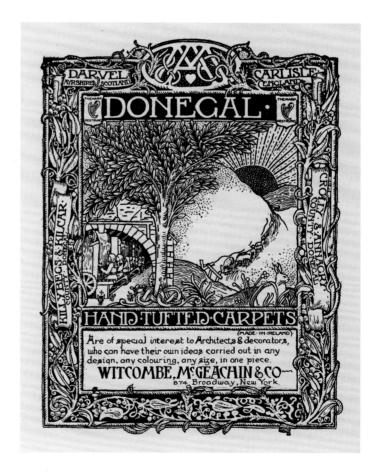

OPPOSITE
The library of the Crab
Tree Cottage at Crab
Tree Farm is furnished
with Stickley furniture,
English textiles, and a
hand-knotted Donegal
rug designed by Gavin
Morton and woven by
Alexander Morton &
Co. in Darvel, Scotland,
1908. See cat. 32.

BELOW
The Rochester,
New York, installation
of Stickley's Arts and
Crafts Exhibition, 1903.
A large Donegal rug is
displayed on the floor.
Courtesy of Rochester
Institute of Technology
Library.

At the same time, he also supplied designs to other manufacturers, notably Tompkinson and Adam of Kidderminster, who made machine-woven floor coverings. Most of Voysey's commercial dealings were contractual and do not seem to have breached technical boundaries. He would sell a design to only one textile printer, textile weaver, or carpet maker, for instance, whereas designs bought by shops that sold a range of furnishings (such as Liberty's) could be used for any type of object that the buyer wished to commission. Donegal carpets were sold in London not only through Liberty & Co. but also Heal & Sons, Goodyers, Storey's, and Maple's and through Wylie & Lockhead in Glasgow and Millar & Beatty in Dublin.

There is no evidence that Voysey sold rug designs to Morton, although he exhibited an original design in the 1899 London Arts and Crafts Exhibition Society exhibition that was cataloged as "executed by Alex. Morton & Co."[56] It is much more likely that the majority of Donegals were adapted from his textile designs. Indeed, *The Craftsman* frequently referred to Donegals as "after the designs of Voysey and his school."[57] James Morton recorded that the designs for early Donegals were taken from Morton's Helena range of textiles. Of the Donegal carpets known to have been designed by Voysey, all were first produced as wallpaper or woven textiles. James Morton also made references in his diary to developing "Voysey-type" designs with Gavin, who ran the firm's design studio, as well as "colouring" Voysey designs with the help of John Llewellyn of Liberty's.

When plans were first made to produce hand-knotted carpets in Ireland in 1897, only two other companies currently produced this work: Yates & Co. and Stephens & Liversedge in Bridgnorth, Shropshire. Donegal carpets were shown at the Irish Arts and Crafts Exhibition of 1899, the Glasgow International Exhibition of 1901, exhibitions held at Liberty's in 1903 and 1907, and the Dublin International Exhibition of 1907. Examples were also exhibited in the United States, in Rochester in 1903 and at the St. Louis Purchase Exposition in 1904, where a demonstration of hand knotting was given by two Irish weavers.

Ready-made Donegal rugs could be purchased throughout the United States from interior designers and furniture stores, including Craftsman shops in New York, Boston, and Washington, D.C., and through *The Craftsman* and Stickley's catalogs. One of the Morton company's strengths was that carpets and rugs could be made on commission to any design, size, or color. This service appealed particularly to interior designers and architects in North America. Custom-designed carpets adorned the official residences of the Governor General of Ottawa, the Saskatchewan Parliament House in Regina, the Arctic Club in Seattle, and the Chicago Athletic Association, which ordered six custom-made carpets in 1909 from Witcombe, McGeachin, & Co.[58]

An advertisement for Donegal rugs in *The Craftsman* in 1906 emphasized the advantage of having a rug made to order, as opposed to "the oriental rug where one has to be satisfied with the nearest size obtainable . . . and frequently [one] has to accept patterns and colorings far from suited to the room."[59]

Cats. 24, 25, 26

Two Hand-Knotted Donegal Rugs and a Runner of the Same Design with Contrasting Borders

Designed by Gavin Morton and G. K. Robertson, before 1899
Woven by Alexander Morton & Co. in Donegal, Ireland,
probably for Liberty & Co., 1899–1905
Hand-knotted in wool (16 knots to the inch) on a woolen warp

Cat. 24
Dark reds, browns, and pale blue on a camel ground with brown border
309.9 × 233.7 cm (122 × 92 in.)
Inscribed on the back: *46180*
PROVENANCE: Malcolm Topalian, New York
Joseph W. Fell, Chicago
Warren Casey, New York
Joseph W. Fell, Chicago, 1996

Cat. 25
Oranges, blues, and greens on a dark blue ground
223.5 × 204.5 cm (88 × 80½ in.)
PROVENANCE: Keshishian, London, 1994

Cat. 26
Orange, red, blues, and green on a dark blue ground with camel colored border
271.8 × 94 cm (107 × 37 in.)
PROVENANCE: Christie's, London, May 1, 1997
Paul Reeves, London, 1997

Malcolm Haslam suggested that early, Eastern-inspired designs like this one may have been initially used by Morton for chenille Axminster carpets. It is not known who Robertson was, though he, with Morton, was identified as the designer of this carpet in the 1901 *Studio Special Summer Number*, which illustrates two versions of the piece on the landing of Dixcot, a London house built and owned by Raleigh Essex, a wallpaper manufacturer. Both carpets have the same border as cat. 24, which is likely to have been the first of these examples used. A Donegal with the same description was exhibited at the London Arts and Crafts exhibition in 1899.[60] LP

Cat. 24

Cat. 25

Cat. 26

Cat. 27

The "Pelican" Hand-Knotted Donegal Rug

Designed by Mary Seton Watts, c. 1889
Hand-knotted by Alexander Morton & Co. in Donegal, Ireland,
for Liberty & Co., 1889–1905
Hand-knotted in wool (16 knots to the inch) on a woolen warp
393.7 × 91.4 cm (155 × 36 in.)
PROVENANCE: Private collection, London
Estate of Sydney Lewis, Virginia
Private collection, Richmond, Virginia
Craftsman Auction, New Jersey, September 27, 2008
Tim Gleason, 2008

The design of this carpet is full of symbolism, denoting the home, secu-
rity, love, and happiness, all of which were continuing themes in the work
of Mary Seton Watts (1850–1938), the second wife of the artist G. F. Watts,
and a noted artist and potter in her own right. James Morton and his wife,
Beatrice, were keen supporters of contemporary artists and makers, and their
friendship with the Wattses led to the commission of terracotta ceramics
by Liberty & Co. and the purchase of carpet designs. The "Pelican" is the only

established design by Watts known to have been put into practice. Exhibited in the 1903 Liberty & Co. exhibition at the Grafton Gallery, it was the only included work in which the designer was named.[61] Furthermore, each symbolic motif was identified in the catalog. A detailed explanation of Celtic art was included in a letter from Watts to the Donegal workers in 1899; it opened with the words "Dear Workers who will tuft this hearth rug."[62] She went on to earnestly emphasize the significance of the pelican, "which will give its own heart's blood to help those who suffer or are in need."[63]

Watts, a Scot by birth, used traditional Celtic patterns in her work. These were copied from surviving early Irish and Scottish stone crosses found in the countryside and illuminated manuscripts such as the medieval Book of Kells, owned by Trinity College Library, Dublin. This style became so fashionable that in 1904 Liberty & Co. housed an exhibition of modern Celtic art that included a number of carpets and rugs by Watts and Archibald Knox (see cats 29 and 30), none of which can be identified from the details in the catalog.

Two variations of this design are known. One, measuring 46 × 103 inches, shows the design in reds and purple on an olive ground.[64] The second version, represented here, has a bottle green ground and is closer to a carpet runner in dimensions. It also has additional borders at each end of a band of Celtic knots.[65] LP

Carpet Runner of the "Fintona" Design Range

Designed in the studio of Alexander Morton & Co. in Darvel, Scotland
(based on an original pattern by C. F. A. Voysey), 1902/03
Hand-knotted by Alexander Morton & Co. in Donegal, Ireland, 1905–10
Hand-knotted wool (20 knots to the inch) on a woolen warp
332.7 × 86.4 cm (131 × 34 in.)
PROVENANCE: Gustav Stickley, New Jersey
Cyril Farny, New Jersey, 1917
Christie's, New York, December 9, 1989
Paul Fiore, Massachusetts, 1989

Copies of Morton records in the Victoria and Albert Museum show two
photographs of commercial textiles with similar designs of large, curving
leaves. One is a machine-woven, flat-weave Caledon carpet at the Victoria and
Albert Museum; the other is a double cloth (at left). This runner exhibits an
expanded border design closely based on the border of the "Fintona" carpet,

TOP TO BOTTOM

Period photograph of a double-cloth furnish-
ing fabric, woven by Alexander Morton & Co.
Courtesy of V & A Images, Victoria and Albert
Museum.

The "Fintona" runner (cat. 28) in front
of a sideboard on the east side of the dining
room in Stickley's home, Craftsman Farms.
Used by permission of The Craftsman Farms
Foundation, Inc.

OPPOSITE

Section of the "Fintona" as shown in *Needle-
Work from the Craftsman Worshops*, 1905.
Courtesy of David Cathers.

one of fifteen Donegals exhibited by Liberty's at their *Irish Hand-Made Carpets* exhibition at the Grafton Gallery, London, in 1903. It is shown in a contemporary *Studio* magazine photograph of the exhibition. Malcolm Haslam identified this design of giant hemlock plants as the "Fintona" from a description in the catalog. He subsequently rescinded this view, although his first assumption seems to have been correct.

Available in the United States through *The Craftsman*, the carpet first appeared as a line drawing in "Living Room: Craftsman House, Series of 1904, Number V." A small sample of the "Fintona" and border also appears in advertisements for Donegal carpets in catalogs from 1905, 1910, and 1912. Stickley purchased two versions of the carpet and this matching runner for the dining room of the Log House at Craftsman Farms. In the November 1911 issue of *The Craftsman*, Natalie Curtis described the carpets: "The colour scheme in the dining room is much the same as the living room except the rugs are brighter in tone, being hand-made Donegal Irish rugs in which yellow design blends with green."[66] An illustration shows the runner in situ. The largest of the carpets is now in the collection of the Metropolitan Museum of Art, New York, and the second has been returned to Craftsman Farm by Crab Tree Farm. LP

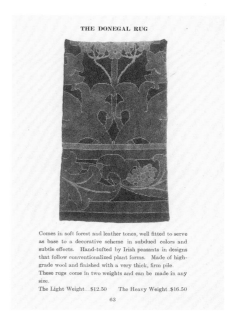

THE DONEGAL RUG

Comes in soft forest and leather tones, well fitted to serve as base to a decorative scheme in subdued colors and subtle effects. Hand-tufted by Irish peasants in designs that follow conventionalized plant forms. Made of high-grade wool and finished with a very thick, firm pile. These rugs come in two weights and can be made in any size.

The Light Weight... $12.50   The Heavy Weight..$16.50

63

Cats. 29, 30

Two Hand-Knotted Rugs of the Same Design

Drawn in the Morton Design Studio and probably based on designs
by Archibald Knox or the Silver Studio, c. 1902
Woven in Donegal, Ireland, 1902–05
Hand-knotted wool (16 knots to the inch) on a wool warp
213.4 × 121.9 cm (84 × 48 in.)

Cat. 29
PROVENANCE: Paul Reeves, London

Cat. 30
PROVENANCE: Averill Harris, Pennsylvania, 1995
Tim Gleason, New York, 1995

These two rugs show the delicacy of coloring and clarity of design that the
best and most skillful Irish carpet weavers could achieve. They also demonstrate the range and subtlety of dyestuffs imported from Germany and
used by Alexander Morton & Co. Both have green woolen warps that give
the surface pile a luminosity characteristic of the best Donegals. A suggested
attribution to Knox is based on a study of his repeating patterns, many of
which have survived. Scottish by parentage and a Manxman (born in the
Isle of Man) by birth, Knox was a prodigious designer who is now credited
with designing most of the Cymric and Tudric ranges of metalwork sold by
Liberty's, although the shop did not identify his work. His connection with
the London Silver Studio has further complicated identification of his work.
He was a friend of Rex Silver, the son of the founder, and it is clear that he
worked for or at the studio. The idiosyncratic, stylized borders of these rugs
are reminiscent of his work, which, like Voysey's designs, may have been
adapted or extracted from a larger pattern by Gavin Morton. LP

Cat. 29

Cat. 30

Machine-Woven Chenille Axminster Carpet

Designed in the Morton Studio (after C. F. A. Voysey and his school)
Manufactured by Alexander Morton & Co. in Darvel, Scotland, c. 1902
Machine-woven chenille Axminster
543.6 × 363.2 cm (214 × 143 in.)
PROVENANCE: Keshishian, London, 2008

This design was used for both hand-knotted Donegals and machine-woven
Axminster carpets. Alexander Morton's son Guy (nicknamed "Big Guy")
was in charge of the production of chenille carpets (which utilize the same
technique as "Patent Axminsters") (see cat. 13); from 1895 these accounted for
nearly a quarter of the firm's total output. Production in Darvel continued
following the establishment of hand-knotting in Ireland, and some patterns
were used for both techniques.

Stickley sold both hand-knotted and machine-woven versions of this
Morton carpet from about 1904. Advertisements in *Craftsman Furnishings* of 1909
and in *Craftsman Furniture* of 1910 and 1912 illustrate the Donegal version of the
pattern, described as in "forest and leather tones of green and brown."[67] LP

An artist's rendering
from *The Craftsman*,
March 1904, of a rug
of the same design
as cat. 31. Rugs that
were on hand in the
Craftsman Building
often served as models
for Stickley's delinea-
tors when they drew
Craftsman House
interiors.

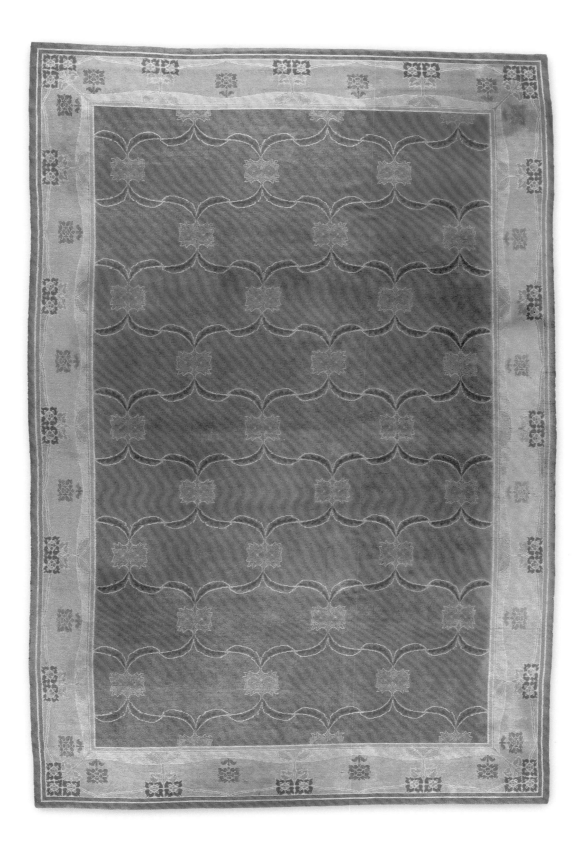

Hand-Knotted Donegal Carpet

Designed by Gavin Morton
Woven by Alexander Morton & Co. in Donegal, Ireland, 1908
Hand-knotted (22 knots to the inch) in wool on a woolen warp
274.3 × 228.6 cm (108 × 90 in.)
PROVENANCE: Sir Evans Davies Jones, Wales
Wynford Vaughn-Thomas, Wales
Keshishian, London, 1992

This is one of three Donegal carpets (two of which are now in the Crab Tree Farm Collection) of the same design commissioned from Liberty's for Pentower, a house overlooking the sea near Fishguard, Wales, built by Sir Evan Davies Jones, a civil engineer and politician. The house was subsequently owned by Wynford Vaughan-Thomas, a Welsh journalist and radio and television presenter.

The use of bold, stylized fruit leaves in green on a red ground provided a simple framework for three versions of the design made for the house, all of which are slightly different. A rug used in the corridor includes a central stem with leaves and fruit on either side, and a small, squarer version displays a central cross of stems. No other versions of the design are known. The pattern shows the designer at his most versatile, and the carpet is of the finest quality available from the Donegal looms. Although Donegals were made in thicknesses of twelve to thirty-six knots per square inch, the majority of those made ranged from fifteen to twenty knots per square inch. LP

Cat. 33

Hand-Knotted Circular Rug

Designed by Lieutenant Noel Simmons
Hand-tufted in Britain, 1918
Hand-tufted wool (16 knots to the inch) on a woolen warp
Diam.: 147.3 cm (58 in.)
PROVENANCE: David Black, London, 1999

This unusual, circular rug shows a very typical, simple design for the period with strong coloring. All that is known about Noel Simmons comes from illustrations of two rugs published posthumously in *The Studio Decorative Art Yearbook* for 1918. Identified by his rank, it is likely that Simmons was killed in World War I. The description of the rug as "hand-tufted" rather than "hand-knotted" suggests that it was made at home, either from a kit or, more likely, by an experienced craftswoman using one of a number of techniques and whatever materials were available. The color and texture of the rug indicate wartime austerity. By 1914 Germany was the main supplier of dyes to Britain, but the war made this trade impossible. The dyes used for this rug show none of the subtle pastel colors of previous dyes, yet they do represent the harsh contrasting palette popular at the time. The Crab Tree Farm Collection includes two other examples of this border design, one rectangular, and one oval. LP

Dun Emer Rugs of Ireland

Linda Parry

THE DONEGAL RUG INDUSTRY'S SUCCESS was based, in large part, on the abundance of cheap labor in the area of Ireland in which the factories were established, as well as on generous funding from the British government. Truer to the spirit of the Arts and Crafts movement was the Dun Emer Guild of Dundrum, near Dublin, set up in 1902 by Evelyn Gleeson. Gleeson was a designer who had studied in London under Alexander Millar, a carpet designer who was also well known in his time as the author of a series of articles on the carpet industry written for *Art Journal*. The Dun Emer Guild was a women's cooperative with the twin goals of helping to alleviate poverty and revitalizing traditional crafts. Gleeson believed that Irish craftswomen should utilize Irish materials "in the making of beautiful things,"[68] and the Guild produced a range of decorative and graphic arts, including hand-knotted rugs. During this period, Ireland was in the midst of its struggle for political and cultural independence from England. The revival of an Irish art based on traditional crafts and local materials was significant because it was at odds with British colonialism. A socialist and patriot, Gleeson represented the ideal Arts and Crafts woman: independent, practical, and talented. As inspiration for her designs, she studied illuminated manuscripts and early Christian art, producing a number of simple and colorful rug designs using Celtic knots and interlacings and zoomorphic patterns (see cat. 34).

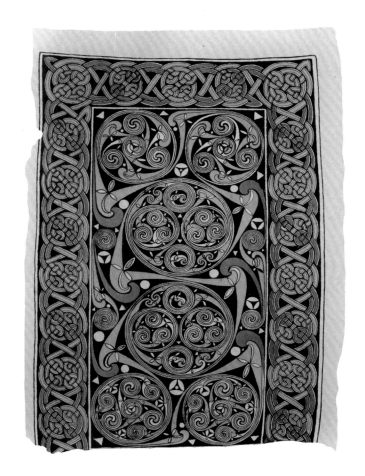

A leaf from the seventh-century *Gospels of Durrow* at Trinity College, Dublin, as reproduced in *Facsimiles of the Miniatures & Ornaments of Anglo-Saxon & Irish Manuscripts Executed by J. O. Westwood* (1868). Courtesy of the Ryerson and Burnham Libraries, Art Institute of Chicago.

OPPOSITE
Detail of cat. 34.

Gleeson became a champion of Irish Arts and Crafts, lecturing and exhibiting the work of Dun Emer internationally, including at a 1908 exhibition in New York. Soon after, *The Craftsman* featured the Guild in an article entitled "The Dun Emer Industries in Ireland: A Successful Example of the Revival of Handicrafts in a Farming Community."[69] It noted that there were far more pressing needs in Ireland than the mere revival of ancient skills: "It is in her farming population that Ireland's salvation lies . . . and the starving condition of these peasants, with the resulting enormous emigration to America of the most progressive among them, is, as Irishmen have long known, a distinct menace."[70]

By instructing the women of the local farming communities in handicrafts, organizations such as the Dun Emer Guild hoped to provide an added source of income to their families, thereby "keeping them contented with their farm life" and providing "another alternative to the two which formerly confronted them — to starve, or go to America."[71]

Gleeson also inspired her niece, Kitty MacCormack, (1892–1975) to design rugs for the Guild. Her work was simpler and more conventional than Gleeson's (see cats. 35 and 36), but it proved popular to a wider Irish market. Dun Emer continued to manufacture carpets until after the end of World War II (see cat. 37).

A Dun Emer label from
the back of cat. 36.

Cat. 34

Hand-Knotted Rug

Designed by Evelyn Gleeson, 1912
Woven in the workshops of the Dun Emer Guild in Dublin, Ireland, c. 1913
Hand-knotted wool (20 knots to the inch) on woolen pile,
with jute binding on a jute warp
175.3 × 121.9 cm (69 × 48 in.)
PROVENANCE: Private Collection, Marblehead, Massachusetts
Private Collection, Boston, Massachusetts
Craftsman Auction, New Jersey, September 20, 2005
Tim Gleason, New York, 2005

Sarah Sherrill illustrated a watercolor design on tracing paper for this carpet, which is inscribed "Hardwicke St / Dublin / Half a carpet."[72] The Dun Emer Guild moved to Hardwicke Street in 1912. This design is part of Gleeson's scrapbook, now in a private collection, and appears to have been developed from an earlier work, a carpet showing a central design of two pelicans, which was exhibited at the 1904 exhibition of the Arts and Crafts Society of Ireland. The earlier rug was illustrated in a 1905 issue of *The Studio*.[73]

From the Guild's inception, Gleeson took control of the tapestry weaving and carpet knotting workshops, which she developed into important local industries that provided work for young girls from the district and used, where possible, the finest quality of local wool. Within two years, she had taken on twelve trainees, two teachers, and six weavers. She also designed most of the carpets woven at Dun Emer from 1902 until about 1920. Her work includes Celtic decoration, often mixed with zoomorphic imagery, as can be seen here. The pelican represents the love and protection of home, and at a time when Ireland yearned for independence, it also acquired symbolic significance (see Watts's design for Liberty's, cat. 27). Nicola Gordon Bowe believed that Gleeson's designs often "reflected the nationalist, socialist, industrial and ultimately political concerns in Ireland which had been gathering momentum since the early years of the nineteenth century."[74] Illegible tags on the back of this carpet may be identification labels. LP

Cat. 35

Hand-Knotted Carpet

Designed by Katherine (Kitty) MacCormack
Woven in the workshops of the Dun Emer Guild in Dublin, Ireland, c. 1920
Hand-knotted wool pile (16 knots to the inch),
with undyed cotton warp and binding wefts
292.1 × 237 cm (116 × 93½ in.)
PROVENANCE: Christie's, South Kensington, May 14, 2002
John Getty, Los Angeles
Christie's, New York, March 9, 2006
Tim Gleason, New York, 2006

Katherine MacCormack was the niece of Evelyn Gleeson. Since childhood MacCormack had lived with her aunt and mother in Runnymede, a house in Dundrum, near Dublin, which in 1902 was renamed Dun Emer and became the headquarters of the Dun Emer Guild. MacCormack is first noted as the designer of ecclesiastical vestments made for the Honan Chapel, Cork, which was consecrated in 1916. In later years, she shared the design and management role at the Guild with her aunt. MacCormack's style is quite different from that of Gleeson. Her work is less figurative or symbolic, with strong, simple patterns in bold colors. From about 1915, the Guild received a number of important national and international commissions, including the carpeting of the hotels and offices of the Canadian and Pacific Railway. Throughout the 1920s and 1930s, orders also came for prestigious Irish buildings, including the library at Leinster House (the Irish Parliament) and the Council Room of the Royal Dublin Society. The carpets made for both of those buildings have strongly architectural designs, as can be seen in this rug, which may also have been ordered for a particular venue. Despite the geometry of the design, it includes cartouches enclosing Celtic motifs. LP

Cat. 36

Hand-Knotted Runner

Probably designed by Katherine (Kitty) MacCormack, probably 1920s
Woven in the workshops of the Dun Emer Guild in Dublin, Ireland
Hand-knotted woolen pile (16 knots to the inch),
with an undyed cotton warp and binding wefts
248.9 × 91.4 cm (98 × 36 in.)
PROVENANCE: Private Collection, Kent, England
Oxford Decorative Arts, Oxford, England, 2002

The use of a vine and grapes in this design, together with a central cruci-
form, suggests that the rug was designed for ecclesiastical purposes and the
composition was woven as an altar carpet. The Dun Emer Guild used this
elongated format, with a central motif and patterned border, frequently, even
with designs showing Celtic decoration. However, secular carpets of this style
are usually wider.

A stencilled label on the back of the rug includes the trademark of Dun
Emer: Celtic knots enclosed within two circles containing the number 0205.
There is also a faint pencil number 57[?]3 on the label, which may refer to
the pattern or the order in which it was woven (see page 96). LP

Cat. 37

Hand-Knotted Carpeting

Probably designed by Katherine (Kitty) MacCormack
Woven in the workshop of the Dun Emer Guild in Dublin, Ireland, after 1945
Hand-knotted woolen pile (16 knots to the inch),
with an undyed cotton warp and binding wefts
594.4 × 322.6 cm (234 × 127 in.) (max.)
PROVENANCE: Craftsman Auction, New Jersey, September 24, 2008
Tim Gleason, New York, 2008

This carpet was almost certainly woven for a church. Its shape suggests
that it would have been placed at the end of the aisle and across the front
of the altar. The simple border design is very similar to orphrey patterns
(edgings on copes or chasubles) embroidered onto vestments, and this carpet
may have been part of a wider ecclesiastical commission. On the back of
the rug is a stencilled Dun Emer label, which bears the hand-written number
4660. On Gleeson's death in 1944, MacCormack took over the Dun Emer
Guild until the 1950s, when the manufacture of rugs ceased. The workshops
finally closed in 1964. LP

Rag Rugs of the Arts and Crafts Era

David Cathers

TECHNICALLY, A RAG RUG is a loom-woven textile with cotton or linen warps and wefts of old cloth cut into strips; such rugs were mostly homemade throughout the nineteenth century. The taste for rag rugs seems to have been well established by about 1905. *American Carpet and Upholstery Journal* observed in 1912 that the revival of these rugs had begun several years before, adding, "Probably no branch of the rug trade has shown longer strides of progress during the past season than the rag rug industry. . . . The public like[s] the 'Colonial' rag rug."[75] The appeal of rag rugs can be attributed to several factors. The Arts and Crafts movement spurred the market for handcrafted wares while also activating a more widespread consumption of factory-made products that had a "handicraft" appearance. The movement also inspired many amateurs to learn a craft and make things for themselves.

Ironically, "modern" developments played a central role in the rag-rug revival. Circular cutting machines and power looms made it possible for carpet factories to turn out large numbers of affordable rag and rag-style rugs, and the industry's sophisticated wholesale and retail distribution system brought those products to consumers nationwide.

OPPOSITE
Detail of cat. 38.

John Wanamaker's "Old Fashioned Rug Shoppe" featured "Colonial rag rugs" in this photograph published in *Carpet and Upholstery Trade Review* in 1909. Courtesy of Art & Architecture Collection, Miriam and Ira D. Wallach Division of Art, Prints, and Photographs, The New York Public Library, Astor, Lenox and Tilden Foundations.

While Stickley did not originate the rag-rug "craze," he was an early and visible advocate of the use of such rugs in domestic interiors. By the time he became involved with rag rugs, many makers were weaving them: individual artisans, small handicraft shops, and large manufactories. The two firms that supplied them to Stickley, however, played particularly important roles in popularizing rag rugs during that era.

Stickley first cataloged rag rugs in *Needle-Work from the Craftsman Workshops*, issued in March 1905. That same month the Craftsman Workshops advertised rag rugs in *The Craftsman*, and the firm continued to market them for at least another ten years. Stickley did not initially refer to these products as rag rugs, though this is evidently what they were. He identified two types in the magazine: "Hand-Woven Rug Number I," said to be made of cotton and priced at $2.50 a square yard; and "Hand-Woven Rug Number II," the material of which was not specified, though it also sold for $2.50 a square yard. A third type featured a geometric central medallion in contrasting colors and was called a "Negamo Rug." It was priced

at $3.25 a square yard, and although the catalog does not specify its material, a trade advertisement confirms that it was made of wool.[76] The catalog also does not identify the makers of these rugs; however, Negamo — a product of the Thread and Thrum Workshop of Auburn, New York — would, within the next few years, become a nationally recognized brand name. Despite Stickley's reticence about identifying his rag rug suppliers, purchase records in his business papers reveal that Thread and Thrum and the American Fabric Rug Company in Philadelphia were his primary suppliers.

Over the years, Negamo or Negamo-like rag rugs were shown in the hallways, living rooms, and dining rooms of many Craftsman houses illustrated in *The Craftsman*, though the magazine generally recommended rag rugs as most suitable for bedrooms. The Negamo rug offered in Stickley's March 1905 textile catalog soon found its way into illustrations in *The Craftsman*. One example is clearly visible in the hall of Craftsman House #4 in the April 1905 issue, and rugs of the same design also appear in Craftsman houses #5 and #6 in the following two

Line drawing of Craftsman House #4, series of 1905, interior with a Negamo rug in the foreground. Published in *The Craftsman*, April 1905.

issues. This is a reminder that rugs that were on hand in the Craftsman Building often served as models for Stickley's delineators when they drew Craftsman houses. It is also a good example of the close connection between Stickley's merchandising efforts in his catalogs and his interior-design recommendations in *The Craftsman*.

The British-born writer and designer Mabel Tuke Priestman (1861–1932), who immigrated to the United States in the early 1890s, enters this story around 1906. At that time, she and her son Gerald noticed that the Thread and Thrum Workshop was successfully selling rag rugs. Those rugs were very like the ones she and her weavers had been making for the past few years; their competitive instincts were apparently stirred, and mother and son established the American Fabric Rug Company. This new firm was soon producing a line of rag rugs with names like "Martha Washington," "John Alden," "Priscilla," and others that evoked America's Colonial heritage.

These products were routinely referred to as hand-woven fabric rugs, though a trade-journal news item in January 1907 reported that the Priestmans had "added new machinery and a new engine, and their production is much greater than heretofore."[77] Like other craft-based firms of the era, including the Craftsman Workshops, the American Fabric Rug Company emphasized its handwork to the public but relied to some extent on machines.

The "Colonial washable rugs for bedroom use" for sale in the Craftsman Building in December 1913 and the rag rugs that Stickley advertised in the June 1914 issue of *The Craftsman* were likely made by the American Fabric Rug Company. When Stickley began shifting his factory's output to Colonial furniture in 1915, some of the photographs of the furniture published in Craftsman advertisements and articles included rag rugs that appear to have been supplied by the American Fabric Rug Company.[78] Despite the magazine's lack of specificity, there is conclusive evidence that Stickley did buy rag rugs made by the firm. His business records at Winterthur document regular purchases from its sales agent, the Germania Importing Company.

RUGS

NEGAMO RUG

These rugs have a uniform back-ground of warm grey and introduce in the center design and the stripes of the border, black, golden browns and terra-cottas.
Woven in various sizes, at . . . . $3.25 per square yard

61

TOP TO BOTTOM

Line drawing of Craftsman House #7, series of 1905, showing a bedroom with a rag rug on the floor. Published in *The Craftsman*, July 1905.

An advertisement for Negamo rugs published in the *Needle-Work from the Craftsman Workshops* catalog, 1905, and priced at $3.25 a square yard. Courtesy of David Cathers.

Cat. 38

Rag Rug

Woven in the United States between 1895 and 1910
Cotton warp, rolled strips of cotton fabric weft, contemporary binding;
overshot weave
152.4 × 86.4 cm (60 × 34 in.)
PROVENANCE: Thomas K. Woodard American Antiques
& Quilts, New York, 2008

Rag carpeting was first introduced to America by the early settlers as an inexpensive and practical floor covering and a way to use fabric scraps that could not be recycled into quilts, garments, or household textiles. Floors were completely covered by lengths cut from a roll and placed side-by-side, often without regard for alignment of the pattern. The lengths were either stitched together and tacked down to the floor along the outside edges, or each length was individually tacked down. The soft, pliant construction often resulted in turned-over edges and corners, and the carpet seldom laid flat.

Early rag carpeting was often woven at home. Even as production moved into the mills in the early twentieth century, companies such as E. C. Beetem, in Carlisle, Pennsylvania, continued using hand-operated looms.[79] This example was cut from a twenty-five-foot-long roll and bound at the two cut edges to make an area rug. DM

Scotch Rugs

David Cathers

SCOTCH RUGS ARE FLAT-WOVEN, reversible wool rugs also known by several other names, including Kilmarnock (after a Scottish town where they were woven), Kidderminster, and ingrain.[80] In April and June 1904, the interiors of Craftsman Houses #4 and #6 were decorated with Scotch rugs; announcing this detail, *The Craftsman* chose not to define the rugs' name for its readers, suggesting that the term was already familiar to both the American carpet trade and American consumers. Scotch rugs were usually imported, though by 1907 a handful of American manufacturers had begun to make and aggressively market them. At that time, Stickley had been selling Morton's machine-woven Caledon rugs (a reversible and inexpensive floor covering) for at least two years; he was one of the trendsetters who helped develop an American market for Scotch rugs.

Though *The Craftsman* mentioned Scotch rugs in 1904, Stickley does not seem to have marketed proprietary Scotch rugs until June 1909, when the magazine advertised the "New Craftsman Rug." This rug was advertised again in the October 1909 issue and offered for sale in *Some Chips from the Craftsman Workshops*, a catalog issued that fall, in time for the Christmas season. The rug was also included in the living room of a Craftsman house illustrated in the magazine in November 1909, though it was not named in the article's text. Made of heavy wool and woven on a power loom, the rug was offered in three colorways: a leaf green ground with the design in "wood and leather tones," a dark brown ground with the design in "lighter wood brown

and straw color," and a dark blue ground with the design "worked in lighter shades."[81] Made in seven sizes—from 36 × 60 inches for $5.00, to 144 × 180 inches for $60.00—it was presented as a perfect rug for a Craftsman interior, and it routinely appeared in the magazine's illustrations of Craftsman houses.

According to the advertisements and catalogs, the innovative design of the "New Craftsman Rug" originated in the Craftsman Workshops. This is a credible claim because an embroidered Craftsman pillow using the same linear and interlacing motifs appeared in the firm's 1909 furniture catalog. Though it evidently survives only in pictures, the rug placed Stickley's firm at the forefront of American Arts and Crafts rug design. Frank Lloyd Wright and the Greene brothers designed custom-made carpets for a few wealthy clients, but with the introduction of this rug, Stickley began selling a high-style, proprietary Arts and Crafts rug that was affordable to a middle-class American market. In this he was going against the broad currents of popular taste. The evidence of trade journals, shelter magazines, and department-store advertisements suggests that the era's status-conscious middle-class consumers preferred to furnish their homes with factory-made Oriental rugs. A handful of American manufacturers did weave Scotch rugs, however, some with geometric patterns, so Stickley was not alone in this market segment. Nonetheless, the "New Craftsman Rug" was a unique textile and one of the Craftsman Workshops' finest creative achievements, though it is largely forgotten today.

OPPOSITE
Detail of cat. 39.

An advertisement from *The Craftsman,* June 1909, for the "New Craftsman Rug," Stickley's proprietary Scotch rug.

Machine-Woven Caledon Carpet or "Art Square"

After a design by C. F. A. Voysey
Woven by Alexander Morton & Co. in Darvel, Scotland, c. 1900
Jacquard machine-woven Kidderminster or inlaid carpet,
with wool warp and weft
406.4 × 172.7 cm (160 × 68 in.)
PROVENANCE: Mr. and Mrs. Herbert Schimmel, New York
R. H. Elllsworth, New York
Sotheby's, New York, June 5, 2001
Tim Gleason, New York, 2001

Usually referred to as Kidderminster or inlaid carpeting, Morton's ranges of flat-woven carpets were named Caledons "because it was the name for something like the old 'Scotch' weave of carpets," according to James Morton.[82] They were also referred to as "Art Squares." This was almost certainly an advertising ploy for Liberty's, which named its fabrics "Art Silks." They were woven on looms purchased from Brintons of Kidderminster, which had attempted to use the looms for chenille carpets without success. *The Art Journal* claimed that Caledons were best used for bedrooms.

This form of reversible, hard-wearing, and inexpensive floor covering eventually became very popular. James and Gavin Morton sought and adapted designs for Caledons. Production expanded and was transferred in 1898 to a factory in Carlisle that was under Gavin's direction. By 1905 sales had suffered, and Caledons never regained their place in the market. This design can be identified from an original photograph of a Caledon in the Victoria and Albert Museum. It has a later pencil attribution to Voysey. There are a number of similar Voysey drawings of birds and trees in the same museum collection. LP

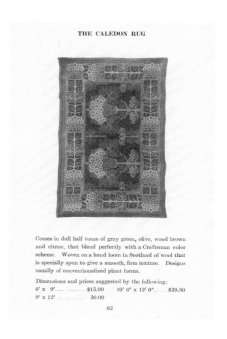

TOP TO BOTTOM

Stickley offered this all-wool Caledon in his needlework catalog in 1905, noting that the designs available in the Caledon range were usually of conventionalized plant forms. Courtesy of David Cathers.

Period photograph of a Caledon carpet sample manufactured by Alexander Morton & Co. Courtesy V & A Images, Victoria and Albert Museum.

Druggets of India

David Cathers

DURING THE SIXTEEN-YEAR LIFE of Stickley's Arts and Crafts enterprise, rugs made in India were extensively imported into the United States. Often designed in England or the United States, they nonetheless were generally thought of as Oriental. According to a book published in 1901, "The best known firms in the rug business in New York, Chicago, and other cities in the United States, and several leading firms in England are sponsors for the present rug industry in India."[83] In 1899 and 1900, Hunter and Witcombe (later to become Witcombe, McGeachin & Co.) imported a large line of Amritzar and Dhuristan rugs, "shown in . . . exclusive designs, and . . . made in India."[84] G. P. and J. Baker, a London manufacturer of printed cottons and later one of Stickley's most important textile suppliers, began importing Indian rugs for the American trade in 1900.[85] The New York–based importer, wholesaler, and department-store retailer Arnold, Constable & Company directed "the designs and color schemes for the entire line" of Indian rugs that it sold to the American trade.[86] Another New York importer, Smead and Lawton, dealt in Indian rugs made to its designs "from our own looms in India."[87] In 1906 Smead & Lawton, Arnold, Constable & Company, and a third New York wholesaler and retailer, W. & J. Sloane, were reported to "control factories in India and transact a very extensive import business in these goods."[88] The H. B. Claflin Company offered Indian rugs and carpets to the trade by 1902.[89]

Of the wide variety of Indian rugs imported into the United States in the early twentieth century, only a small percent were druggets. The story of these imports seems straightforward enough, but it resists tidy analysis. In his "Notes and Comments" column in the February 1903 issue of *House Beautiful*, Oliver Coleman wrote, "From Boston come excellent wool rugs, called India druggets. . . . There is a center of grayish yellow homespun, sprinkled regularly with conventional figures in yellow and red-brown outlined in black. There is a border . . . of red-brown and black well combined . . . both sides are exactly alike."[90] This sounds very like the Craftsman rug that Stickley would later call the Nile drugget. Coleman was unclear about the source of the druggets he described, and it is not known if they were simply retailed in the Boston area or also made there. The question of whether these rugs were imported or domestic raises tantalizing possibilities, though the more important point is that there was a thriving American market for Indian rugs around the turn of the century, and that Stickley was among the early retailers to sense this trend.

A drugget is a weft-faced, flat-woven, reversible rug made with cotton warps and wool wefts and dyed with synthetic dyes. According to *The Craftsman*, the druggets that Stickley imported were "firm, heavy, hand-woven rugs, made especially for us in India."[91]

As his catalogs and magazine show, Stickley and his designers saw that the subdued colors, rugged texture, and rectilinear design motifs of Indian druggets were perfect complements to the coordinated Craftsman interior. They also gave the firm another opportunity to help readers tastefully decorate their homes by buying Craftsman products. In October 1911, *The Craftsman* published "Craftsman Furnishings for the Ordinary Room," a marketing-oriented article illustrated with appealing drawings of a living room, library, and hall. As it explained, "When furniture is ordered from the Craftsman shops a color scheme including the fittings of the

OPPOSITE
Detail of cat. 42.

OVERLEAF
One of two rooms in the Old Garage and Stables at Crab Tree Farm. This room features druggets and Stickley furniture.

In Craftsman House #7 (July 1904), the drawing of the library shows a Nile drugget with two parallel zigzag lines running through its border. The text does not identify the rugs in this house as druggets, noting only that "the rugs used, with one exception, are of goat's hair in gray, brown, deep red and orange yellow; the exception being an old-time 'rag rug' lying between the library and dining room."[94] In the 1904 booklet "What is Wrought in the Craftsman Workshops," four Stickley needle-workers are shown plying their craft in a room with an apparently identical Nile drugget on the floor, though the rug is not mentioned in the text. This photograph is important because it documents the presence of at least one drugget in the Craftsman Building by 1904.

The March 1905 Craftsman needlework catalog pictures an Indian drugget said to be woven of camel's hair and described as follows: "The main body is grey, either plain or with a geometrical pattern in old yellow, brown and russet. The border of dull red shows a zig-zag pattern in dark brown."[95] The description does not say it is reversible. Sizes and prices started at 60 × 48 inches for $10.75 and rose to 216 × 168 inches for $120. Though designated "India Carpet," and then "India Rug" in subsequent catalogs, this rug was offered essentially unchanged through 1909. In late 1905 or early 1906, it was priced at $2.50 a square yard, and by 1908 it had nearly doubled in price to $4.75 a square yard. These catalogs do not say who designed the India rug, nor is the phrase "Made in India" included in the descriptions. Indeed, nothing is said about where it was made, and keeping Coleman's *House Beautiful* article in mind, it is not known whether this rug was imported or domestic. By the time Stickley's firm issued its 1910 furniture catalog, its druggets had been given the names by which they are known today: Nile and Scroll.

Although druggets seem to be the only Craftsman floor coverings to have survived, very little was known about them until recent research revealed the general outline of their origins. As Sarah Sherrill wrote, the Nile pattern is in fact a "traditional design, woven in Walajapet village, Tamil Nadu (formerly Madras) State, southeastern India."[96] The Scroll rug also uses a traditional design from the same part of India, "an Islamic India star-and-cross interlace field pattern."[97] In Craftsman catalogs

room, the fabrics, etc., will always be furnished upon application."[92] The living room illustrated in the article, decorated in various shades of brown, included a Nile rug: "On the floor is a large rug (9 × 12 feet, $57), one of the beautiful India druggets which the Craftsman imports from India. This is in shades of brown with the figures outlined in black. We find these India druggets especially beautiful in relation to Craftsman furniture and quite as durable." In the mostly brown and gray-green hall, "the rug ($28.50) is an India drugget with home-spun background and scroll design of green which harmonizes beautifully with the other touches of green in the hall."[93]

issued from 1905 through 1909, these rugs were said to be made of camel's hair. Then a change took place. According to catalogs of 1910 through 1912, as well as Stickley's advertisements in *The Craftsman* from 1911 through 1913, Nile and Scroll druggets were constructed of bullocks' wool. Sherrill identified these rugs as weft-faced, plain-weave druggets, with cotton warps and wool wefts, and added that the wool was poor-quality sheep's wool, dry and brittle. As she wrote, the camel's hair and bullocks' wool designations "may have been based on an importer's misconceptions, or on a desire to obscure a decidedly unprestigious type of wool." In her view, many of Stickley's claims about his druggets were "demonstrably salesmanship."[98]

Sherrill's analysis of Stickley's druggets is very enlightening, but important additional information can be found in the era's trade journals. In February and March 1912, the Kilmarnock Textile Manufacturing Company advertised a new product in *American Carpet and Upholstery Journal*. The February advertisement announced the "Kilmarnock entry in a new field. . . . The reproduction of the Indian Drugget . . . made almost perfect to the Originals on account of the similarity in texture."[99] It boasted that "the Best Houses [retailers] in the country are featuring them this season."[100] The photograph illustrating this advertisement shows a Nile drugget, apparently identical to the version that Stickley first cataloged in 1910. In the firm's March advertisement, this same photograph was captioned "One of the New Indian Drugget Designs," evidence that this was not the only drugget offered by Kilmarnock. These druggets were probably made of the same wool that the firm used in its Scotch rugs, though the advertisement does not say so.

The Kilmarnock Company produced druggets for at least two years. In its February 10, 1914, *American Carpet and Upholstery Journal* advertisement, it depicted one on the floor of a Craftsman-like room and offered reproducible line art to retailers for advertising use. Kilmarnock most likely began manufacturing druggets — including one with the Nile design — because its managers knew from their contacts with Stickley that those rugs were selling well. This might explain why Stickley druggets are relatively easy to find today: some surviving examples are no doubt the firm's products, while others have nothing to do with it and came instead from

Kilmarnock. This further suggests that the druggets occasionally visible in non-Craftsman interiors photographed for the era's shelter magazines might have come from Stickley or from some other retailer that carried Kilmarnock's rugs.

TOP TO BOTTOM

Advertisement for a Kilmarnock rug from the *American Carpet and Upholstery Journal*, February 1912, showing a drugget. Courtesy of Art & Architecture Collection, Miriam and Ira D. Wallach Division of Art, Prints, and Photographs, The New York Public Library, Astor, Lenox and Tilden Foundations.

The living room at Craftsman Farms, Stickley's home, c. 1911, with a Scroll drugget on the floor. Used by permission of the Craftsman Farms Foundation, Inc.

Cat. 40

Nile Drugget

Made in India, 1904/16
Cotton warp, wool weft
297.2 × 251.5 cm (117 × 99 in.)
PROVENANCE: Treadway/Toomey Galleries, Oak Park, Illinois
Tim Gleason, New York

Though Stickley briefly offered other druggets, the two he routinely sold were the Nile and Scroll druggets, his firm's name for what were in fact standard Indian patterns.[101] Nile druggets have a dark border with a zigzag motif running through it, and in the center, there are rhythmically placed geometric motifs arrayed on a neutral ground. Such rugs were offered in several colorways. According to the description of a similar rug shown in the firm's 1906 textile catalog, "The main body is gray . . . with a geometrical pattern in old yellow, brown and russet. The border of dull red shows a zigzag pattern in dark brown."[102] Two Nile druggets were illustrated in the October 1911 issue of *The Craftsman*, one said to be "in shades of brown with the figures in the center and a border outlined in black," and the other having "a natural toned background and the design . . . carried out in soft tones of copperish browns and dull blue."[103] This drugget has a tan field with russet and old yellow geometric shapes outlined in black; the shapes are created by the insertion of discontinuous wefts. A dull red double zigzag motif runs through the black border, and geometric yellow details accent each corner.

Beginning in 1905, Stickley cataloged the Nile drugget in four sizes, starting with 5 × 4 feet for $10.75 and going up to 18 × 14 feet for $120. Around 1906 it was sold by the yard, and by 1909, the Nile drugget was cataloged as "made in any size."[104] From 1910 on, the available sizes were standardized, with a Nile drugget of 3 × 3 feet priced at $5.50, and a version of 12 × 15 feet, the largest size, available for $95.00. The modest prices of the small and midsize druggets kept them affordable to Stickley's design-conscious middle-class customers.

Though the firm did not evidently apply the name Nile to this pattern until about 1910, rugs of this design were in Stickley's Syracuse, New York, Craftsman Building as early as 1904, and a Nile drugget is also visible in a drawing published in *The Craftsman* from that year. Nile druggets continued to appear in *Craftsman* photographs as late as 1915, reliably indicating that the firm carried these products for at least twelve years. DC

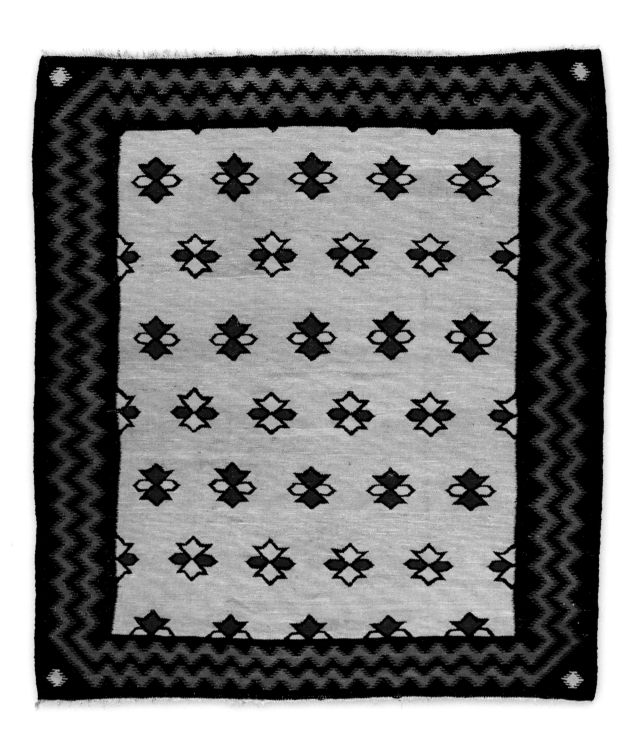

Cat. 41

Scroll Drugget

Made in India, 1912/16
Cotton warp, wool weft
355.6 × 279.4 cm (140 × 110 in.)
PROVENANCE: Treadway/Toomey Auction, Oak Park, Illinois, May 15, 1994
Paul Fiore, 1994

Stickley's firm first carried Scroll druggets in 1910. Although Scroll was the firm's name for this pattern, it is a traditional Islamic interlaced star and cross motif that was created with diagonal and interlocking vertical joins of different colored weft strands.[105] Stickley must have particularly liked this design because he used three large green and gray Scroll druggets in the living room of his home at Craftsman Farms.

Along with the Nile drugget, the Scroll drugget was offered in Stickley's 1910 furniture catalog "in colors and patterns made especially for us, and carefully designed with reference to its harmony with Craftsman furnishings."[106] A Scroll drugget shown in a drawing of a Craftsman interior in the October 1911 issue of *The Craftsman* was described as having a "homespun background and a scroll design of green which harmonizes beautifully with the other touches of green in the hall."[107] The firm's marketing of druggets consistently emphasized this theme of design unity. Moreover, the deft use of the word *homespun* downplayed the druggets' foreign pedigree and evoked the sturdy domestic virtues of the American Colonial Revival.

The Scroll drugget was initially offered with a plain band border and made in three colorways: a green scroll and border on a plain ground; a blue scroll and border on a plain ground; and a light-colored scroll and border on a green and blue ground. It was later available with black scrolls and border on a golden-brown ground. By 1912 it was cataloged with blue scrolls on a natural tan-colored ground or, like the present example, with green scrolls and border on a tan ground. Beginning that year, the larger sizes of the Scroll druggets were cataloged with either a plain band or a Greek key border. On the basis of that evidence, this example from the Crab Tree Farm Collection probably dates to 1912/16.

From 1912 through at least 1914, the Kilmarnock Textile Manufacturing Company of Philadelphia manufactured reproduction Indian druggets. The few druggets Kilmarnock illustrated in its trade-journal advertisements appear identical to Stickley's Nile druggets, though this Pennsylvania rug maker produced other patterns as well. Stickley was a steady Kilmarnock customer, evidently buying the Scotch rugs they also manufactured, and the routine contact between the two firms may have led Kilmarnock to introduce its own line of druggets. It is likely that some Stickley druggets known today are machine-woven Kilmarnock products made in the United States. DC

<u>Cat. 42</u>

Scroll Runner

Made in India, 1912/16
Cotton warp, wool weft
269.2 × 71.1 cm (106 × 28 in.)
PROVENANCE: Robert Kaplan, New York
John Toomey Gallery, Oak Park, Illinois, 2001

In 1910, the year it was first cataloged, the Scroll drugget was offered in six standard sizes, starting with a rug of 3 × 3 feet for $5.50 and rising to a rug of 12 × 15 feet for $95. In 1912, perhaps in an effort to stimulate sales, the firm reduced the prices of all its Scroll druggets, with the smaller size now

priced at $4.50 and the larger size dramatically dropped to $72. By early 1913, however, Stickley's rug advertisements in *The Craftsman* show that his Scroll drugget prices had reverted to their higher 1910 levels. The prices of other Stickley rugs generally held steady or fell slightly from 1910 to 1912, and the reasons for the fluctuations in price of the Scroll druggets remain unclear.

In 1912 new Scroll drugget sizes were introduced. The entry in the Craftsman catalog of that year, *Craftsman Furnishings for the Home*, noted, "These are also made in narrower widths and any length for hall runners, prices of which will be furnished upon application."[108] On the evidence of that promotional copy, this green and beige example in the Crab Tree Farm Collection likely dates from 1912/16 and would have been initially purchased as a special order. DC

Navajo Rugs of the Southwestern United States

Diane Boucher

THE IDEA OF A COUNTRY promoting its identity through the arts can be traced back to the nineteenth-century Romantic movement in Europe. The artists and architects of Romanticism sought inspiration for their architectural styles and subject matter from the historical and mythological past. For British and European designers and craftsmen, the wealth of history and folklore in their homelands provided them with an abundance of appropriate motifs and styles. But how could the newly created United States, with its disparate immigrant population and diverse geographic area, fashion a national identity based on a historic past? This was the question that a variety of contributors to *The Craftsman* sought to answer. The comments of George de Szögyénÿ, the Commercial Commissioner of the Royal Hungarian Government, are typical of those of many writers in their criticism of the overreliance of American artists on European models. He lamented, "There is handwork done in America . . . but it does not seem in any way expressive of American life or character as both design and workmanship seem almost invariably to be derived from foreign sources."[109] The author did, however, make one exception — Native American art, which he described as "the only American handicrafts so far that are made to supply everyday needs and that therefore are a genuine expression of primitive art."[110]

Native Americans were North America's only truly indigenous people. It was, therefore, inevitable that the American Arts and Crafts movement looked to them for inspiration in the search for "a national spirit in art."[111] *The Craftsman* carried many articles on the subject by ethnologists, artists, and even Stickley himself. Generally, the writers adopted a nostalgic view of Native American cultures, bemoaning their

"extinction" and admiring their unique link to the past — a simple preindustrial lifestyle "possessing crafts, arts, a system of morals and a religious faith not to be despised."[112] One article stated: "They belong to our own country and are part of our historical inheritance, so that the same spirit which prompts us to search genealogical records, and to attempt to locate the habitat from which our ancestors migrated, should inspire us with interest and love for American antiquities."[113] Another contributor, praising Native American craftsmanship for both its utility and its beauty, wrote that it was "the only real handicraft this country knows," since it was inspired by "the spontaneous growth of necessity and therefore an absolutely natural expression of the individuality of the maker."[114]

Photograph from the November 1903 issue of *The Craftsman*, showing a Navajo woman at a loom.

OPPOSITE
Detail of cat. 45.

OVERLEAF
The interior of the Lodge at Crab Tree Farm featuring a number of Navajo blankets and rugs. Photo by Craig Dugan, Hedrich-Blessing.

Contributors to *The Craftsman* sought practical ways to promote Native American artifacts by educating tribes in the revival of their lost arts, "such as the old use of vegetable dyes and the ancient method of glazing pottery, and so give [the Indian] better facilities for working at his own primitive, beautiful crafts."[115] They hoped that, as a result of this artistic revival, the Native American artisan would find "a ready market for his fabrics, baskets and pottery made and decorated after the ancient manner of his race," instead of producing "hideous, commercial trash."[116] A 1906 *Craftsman* article described the transfer of Native American crafts to the rest of the United States: "The Navajo blankets have a worldwide fame, and those of native wool and dyes made by the Indians are often of beautiful design and very expensive. . . . Bales are sent in from the country, piled on the backs of burros, stored in the warehouses of way-stations and finally sent to Los Angeles, San Francisco, New York, Chicago and other large centers for goods of this character."[117]

Native American rugs were marketed by traders in a number of ways: The best quality rugs made for John Lorenzo Hubbell (1853–1930) were sold through the Fred H. Harvey Company for prices ranging from $40 to $150. The company owned the hotel concession operating along the Santa Fe railroad, and in several of the hotels, they had "Indian rooms" where Navajo rugs and other

Native American products could be purchased. Local fairs provided the weavers with another important opportunity to display their finest wares. These were mainly held in popular tourist areas such as Santa Fe and Taos, and they drew support not only from the tourists but also from the artists and writers who were attracted to the area in the early twentieth century.

The main selling techniques for Native American crafts on the East Coast included the use of advertisements in "lifestyle" magazines, such as *The Craftsman*, and the new mail-order catalogs. Clinton N. Cotton (1859–1936) produced the first catalog of Navajo rugs in 1896, and Hubbell published his first in 1902. All of the advertisers of Navajo rugs in *The Craftsman* emphasized the genuine nature of their particular stock and the uniqueness of each design. Francis E. Lester of Mesilla Park, New Mexico, was a frequent advertiser. In January 1912, Lester's advertisement read:

> For fifteen years I have been selling genuine Indian rugs direct from Indian weaver to customer. I live among the Indians themselves. I have in my employ expert weavers from families famous for generations for their perfect rug work. Every rug I sell is woven entirely by hand from pure native wool, hand-clipped and hand cleaned by the Indians; then hand-spun on primitive spinning wheels and dyed in primitive fashion by their slow, painstaking process that gives the genuine Indian rug its rich lasting colors.[118]

A. M. Starmont and Son of Thompson, Utah, advertising in 1913, offered rugs "made in the open air, with the crudest of weaving methods, by wise old women who carry the designs in their heads. Rugs no two of which are alike; rugs which a white man never sees until a straight and stalwart Navajo sells them to our traders for a pile of silver half-dollars."[119]

Navajo rugs and other Native American artifacts could be bought in major department stores, including Stickley's twelve-story emporium just off Fifth Avenue in New York. A December 1914 *Craftsman* article entitled "The American Santa Claus and His Gifts" featured American Arts and Crafts products sold in the store and suitable for holiday gifts. These included "some remarkably interesting Indian rugs and baskets, lamp shades and leather work, with all

An advertisement for Francis Lester's company that appeared in the November 1907 issue of *The Craftsman*.

This Beautiful Hand-Woven Indian Rug

Direct from Indian Weaver to You
Delivered FREE on 3 Days' Approval

I have been selling genuine Indian blankets, **direct from the Indian Weaver to the customer**, for the past 15 years. Because I sell only genuine goods (I never sold an imitation), at about ½ regular values, my business has grown until it is today known as the largest of its kind in the world. The blankets I sell are entirely **hand-woven** by the best Navajo and Pueblo Indian weavers of their tribes, from pure, native wool, hand-clipped by the Indians from their own sheep, and entirely handspun. I want every reader of *Craftsman* to know more of this beautiful handicraft of my Indians and I therefore make this

Special Craftsman Offer

The Indian rug here illustrated is a masterpiece of fine Indian weaving. It is the handiwork of one of my best Pueblo weavers, an expert, whose forefathers have been weaving blankets for 100 years. It is **woven under my personal supervision** and every strand of it is pure native handspun wool. It measures 30 by 60 inches. The design is an original Indian figure in lightning and ceremonial cross pattern. I can send you the rug in any of 3 shades, the design in black and white, with the ground color in either a deep rich red, a dark olive green, or a deep Indian blue. The weave is close and heavy, just right for floor use, and the rug will literally **last a life-time**. No illustration can do justice to its soft coloring and rare handiwork.

I want to send you this rug on 3 days' approval. Its regular retail value is $18.00, but upon receipt of your check, draft or money order for **$10.00** I will deliver the rug to your address all **express charges prepaid**. Place the rug in your home and if at the end of 3 days you are not delighted with it, return it at my expense and I will refund the $10.00 paid. Isn't this fair?

If your order is received this month, with this special offer attached, I will send you FREE with each rug ordered a $2.00 **Zuni Indian Basket**, 13 inches wide, or a $2.00 Indian Pottery Bowl. Order today and state color of rug desired.

If interested in Indian blankets, write me **today** for my special art catalog showing Indian blankets in actual colors, regular price 10 cents, but sent FREE in answer to this ad. Send today.

Francis E. Lester, Pres. FRANCIS E. LESTER CO., Dept. AV 56, Mesilla Park, New Mexico
Largest Retailers of Indian and Mexican Handicraft in the world.

the rich coloring and wonderful craftsmanship for which this work is famed." [120]

In 1903 Stickley set up a fabric and needlework department and design studio. Craftsman textiles included cushions, curtains, portières, and table runners. These were usually made from open-weave linens, using basic embroidery stitches, appliqué, or stenciling. In conjunction with the department, *The Craftsman* promoted these textiles — which could be purchased either in kit form (to include all materials) or as finished products — through articles and advertisements. Stickley's introduction of a textile department was an important step in his plan to create an integrated Craftsman interior — a combination of forms, textures, and colors that would be "pleasing and restful."

Simple, stylized patterns, derived from Native American crafts, featured in a number of designs. Examples can be seen in three Craftsman canvas pillows believed to be the work of Harvey Ellis, which were "embroidered with North American motifs derived . . . from the basketry and pottery of the Pueblo tribes." [121] *The Craftsman* likened the use of these motifs to "the Briton and Celtic systems, which are now in active, enthusiastic revival in England furthered alike by the guilds and by individual artists and craftsmen." [122] Not everyone, however, agreed that these designs were appropriate for house furnishings. Fred H. Daniels, director of drawing in the public schools of Springfield, Massachusetts, took exception to the pillow designs in a letter to the magazine: "A bear, a deer, or a pine tree, has no more symbolic relation to your home life or mine than a roll-top desk would have to a Pueblo Indian. Such symbols are entirely out of place in our homes." [123] Despite this criticism, *The Craftsman* soldiered on in its attempt to introduce the idea of decorating homes with Native American furnishings and motifs to its readers.

Navajo rugs were used in Craftsman interiors to add bright color notes, texture, and a sense of authenticity. They were found in rustic lodges and summer homes and the more informal spaces of American Arts and Crafts houses, such as dens, porches, and garden rooms.

Craftsman homes often incorporated porches designed as a link between the garden and the house. *The Craftsman* explained these outdoor living rooms:

It goes without saying that the furniture should be plain and substantial, fitted for the more rugged outdoor life and able to stand the weather. Indian rugs or Navajo blankets lend a touch of comfort and cheer, and the simple designs and primitive colors harmonize as well with trees and vines and the open sky as they do with their native wigwams. If the sunlight is too strong, the rolling shade of Japanese split bamboo is not only useful but decorative in these outdoor rooms, and willow chairs and settles seem to belong naturally to life in the garden. [124]

A vacation bungalow built of fieldstone and designed to "harmonize with the natural environments of its location by the shore, the mountains or the forest dale" [125] was featured in the March 1905 issue of *The Craftsman*. The magazine recommended that readers keep the arrangement of the main living space simple, but "small accessories to effect a color-scheme may be added in the form of Indian blankets, bright pillows, copper utensils and hand-wrought andirons." [126]

Charles A. Eastman, a Native American, wrote in a 1914 article: "It is the quality of sincerity that gives the Indian blanket its peculiar value when used as a rug, portière or couch cover in a Craftsman room. . . . No form of drapery harmonizes quite so well with plain, sturdy forms in woodwork and furniture and with the mellow tones of natural wood, as do these Indian blankets, for the reason that they are simply another expression of the same idea." [127] A particularly fine example of just such a harmonious relationship between Indian rugs and Craftsman furnishings was Illahee, a country house that was based on one of the Craftsman house designs. It was built near Hayden Lake, deep in the Idaho National Forest. The owner of Illahee, an Indian word meaning "home by lake," was inspired to build his country home following a visit to Lake Como in Italy. He did not, however, want an Italian-influenced design, selecting instead "one that would be a perfect expression of himself and his country." [128] His choice was a Craftsman house design, modified to suit his family's requirements. The house incorporates Craftsman furnishings and a selection of Navajo rugs.

Interiors of Illahee, a house in the Idaho National Forest, featured in *The Craftsman* in October 1916.

Cat. 43

Navajo Transitional Blanket or Rug

(Revival Serape Style)

Likely exchanged or sold by the weaver to Hubbell Trading Post, Navajo Reservation, Ganado, Arizona, late 19th–early 20th century
Hand-woven rug made with hand-carded and hand-spun native wool; natural wool colors and synthetic dyed red wool
125.7 × 86.4 cm (49½ × 34 in.)
PROVENANCE: Second Phase Gallery, Taos, New Mexico, 1998

For several centuries, Navajo weavers created blankets that clothed their families and served as goods to trade with other tribes. Their "wearing blankets," or serapes, often had three to five zones of patterning, with each end divided into three dominant motifs. In this textile, a weaver copied the zoned blanket style, but incorporated sharply serrated motifs common after the 1880s, rather than using the stepped, or terraced, elements that prevailed in blankets before 1880. Indeed, Navajo weavers rarely imitated a model exactly and always preferred to vary their woven work.

Indian trader Cotton would have called this a "Fancy Blanket," made after hand-woven wearing blankets had fallen out of fashion and Navajos began acquiring commercial trade blankets for their own use. In 1896 he wrote:

> These blankets are woven from native wool, dyed in fancy colors, are very pretty, and are used as rugs, robes, portières, hangings, etc. The higher priced ones are of scarlet ground, with fancy designs in high colors. . . . No two are alike in design. Many prefer them to the most expensive blanket, as they are more strictly Navajo, the wool being dyed, spun and woven entirely by the natives. Prices, $5.00, $7.00, $8.00, $10.00, $12.00 and $15.00 each.[129]

Cotton's influence on Navajo weaving and its widespread popularity at the turn of the twentieth century is often overlooked. His first catalog picturing hand-woven rugs was published in 1896 and preceded both J. L. Hubbell's and J. B. Moore's efforts to reach East Coast and Midwest collectors. Starting as Hubbell's partner in 1884, Cotton gained full interest in their famous trading post at Ganado in 1885, operating it himself until 1900. (Hubbell bought the post back around 1902 and continued there until his death in 1930.) Beginning in 1888, Cotton was also the major wholesaler of Indian goods in Gallup, New Mexico. He distributed to dealers and collectors — from Pasadena and Berkeley to Chicago and New York — who were aficionados of the Arts and Crafts movement. ALH

Cat. 44

Navajo Transitional Blanket or Rug

(Germantown Yarns)

Likely exchanged or sold by the weaver to Hubbell Trading Post,
Navajo Reservation, Ganado, Arizona, late 19th–early 20th century
Hand-woven rug made with commercial four-ply mill-spun Germantown wool
yarn; synthetic dyes; handspun, natural-colored white and indigo-dyed
dark blue native wool
210.8 × 134.6 cm (83 × 53 in.)
PROVENANCE: American Renaissance Gallery, Santa Fe, New Mexico, 1998
Tim Gleason, New York, 1998

This tightly woven blanket or rug was never meant to be worn as a shoulder
blanket. The weaver probably sold or traded it to a trading post almost
as soon as it left the loom. The sale of such textiles — transitional in style,
weight, and function between wearing blankets and floor rugs — was a main-
stay for Navajo households at the turn of the twentieth century, as Native
American families moved from barter to a cash economy. Buyers interested
in these rugs sought "authentic" and even "primitive" Indian goods just as,
ironically, they were supporting changes to the Navajo lifestyle.

The careers of some Navajo weavers spanned several stylistic periods.
Perhaps the weaver of this transitional piece wove wearing blankets earlier
in life and then switched to weaving rugs for sale to outsiders. The handling
of materials, firmly twined edging cords, and balanced design attest to traditional qualities in the work. The rug incorporates tightly respun commercial
wool yarn that came from Eastern mill towns. The best-known factories
that shipped yarns to Navajo country were in Germantown, Pennsylvania.
Therefore, yarns and textiles of this type are now known generically as
Germantowns. Hubbell Trading Post sold several types of commercial yarns
and synthetic dyes to local weavers at the turn of the century; Germantowns
appear in the Hubbell records into the second decade of the twentieth
century. This weaver used both commercial yarns and hand-spun wool.

The weaver of this blanket created overall zigzags by weaving a series
of small squares in a "stair-step" manner. Although earlier wearing blankets
also have stepped patterns, this unified allover treatment is a turn-of-the-
century development. In fact, this exact design appears in a 1905 painting that
Chicago artist Elbridge Ayer Burbank (1858–1948) made for Hubbell; the
small artwork was meant as a model for local weavers and depicts
a saddle blanket with a red ground and a black-and-white zigzag pattern
of squares.[130] ALH

Navajo Transitional Rug

("Eye Dazzler" Style)

Likely exchanged or sold by the weaver to Crystal Trading Post, Navajo Reservation, Crystal, New Mexico, late 19th–early 20th century
Hand-woven rug made with hand-carded and hand-spun wool; native sheep's wool in natural white and gray, synthetic top-dyed black, and synthetic dyed red
228.6 × 137.2 cm (90 × 54 in.)
PROVENANCE: White Bear Rug Company, Highland Park, Illinois, 1998

During the late nineteenth century, Navajo weavers adapted patterns from Mexican and Hispanic blankets for their own rugs. The classic Saltillo serape from northern Mexico provided a prototype for many Navajo weavers. Saltillo influences included sharply serrated zigzag motifs, a vertically stacked orientation of designs, and diagonally patterned borders. (Navajo weavers also borrowed border patterns from Oriental carpets and elsewhere.) This transitional rug illustrates all of these Mexican serape traits. Somewhere along the line, a trader began calling this type of design an "eye dazzler," an apt description that stuck.

Deeply serrated diamonds and zigzags integrated into an allover pattern were featured in trader J. B. Moore's 1911 catalog. Discussing a borderless variation of this serrated pattern, Moore wrote, "The pattern is one of the most typical and generally worked of any we show. Almost half of [this] class of rugs are woven in some variation of it, and have always been. . . . Frequently a border is woven around, and this also gives the rug a more finished and complete appearance." [131]

Early "eye dazzlers" often contained many varied colors from synthetic dyes. The palette of this rug, limited to natural sheep's colors and synthetic red dye, suggests that it was made between 1900 and 1915. Collectors attuned to an Arts and Crafts sensibility generally preferred rugs with fewer and more basic colors, such as this example. From 1902 until 1913, Adeline P. Alcutt, the proprietress of the Wigwam Shop in Pasadena, California — where Craftsman-oriented taste reigned — placed orders with Hubbell Trading Post, proclaiming, "The bright Indian Dye blankets do not sell in a place like Pasadena." [132] She repeatedly requested "black and white, that beautiful darker red and grey, and grey white with a touch of red." [133] "The Germantowns — good colors especially the old style and some of the chief blankets — the brilliant colors — purples greens, browns, etc. do not sell here — The demand is for the very best, wool warp[,] grays, reds and dark blues and black and white," explained Alcutt. [134] ALH

Cat. 46

Navajo Rug

(Style influenced by J. L. Hubbell)

Likely exchanged or sold by the weaver to Hubbell Trading Post,
Navajo Reservation, Ganado, Arizona, late 19th–early 20th century
Hand-woven rug made with hand-carded and hand-spun wool; native sheep's
wool in natural white and gray, synthetic top-dyed black, and synthetic dyed red
194.3 × 162.6 cm (76½ × 64 in.)
PROVENANCE: Edward R. Varndell, Chicago, 1997

Many turn-of-the-century buyers sought rugs with traditional Indian motifs. Trading partners Hubbell and Cotton responded by favoring large-scale motifs abstracted from earlier Navajo blanket styles. The two equal-armed crosses within a double diamond were motifs borrowed from late classic wearing blankets, in which small, repeated crosses and diamonds were common. This pairing appears in a number of 1905 rug paintings at Hubbell Trading Post made by Burbank when he traveled west. The serrated edging here was a common addition. Hubbell and Cotton also encouraged Navajo weavers to use simple, unpatterned borders.

Displaying native curios and textiles such as this in an Indian room, corner, or "den" was popular among many collectors in the Midwest and on the East Coast around the turn of the twentieth century. Quite a few visited and corresponded with Hubbell Trading Post. R. N. Stites, a Chicago business executive, wrote in December 1904: "I was away on a little hunting trip . . . at camp, which is at State Line, Wisconsin. . . . I wish that you would send me six kachenis [sic] — those little Moque [Hopi] dolls. I would like . . . the best that you can get."[135] In July 1905, he reported to Hubbell: "Going back to the Katchinas — they were just what I wanted, exactly. I have stood them on the picture molding, over my little Indian collection, and it sets it off in great shape."[136] Another Chicagoan, W. S. Wilber, wrote to Hubbell asking for Indian blankets and other merchandise: "I have a farm at Tomahawk, Wisconsin, which is in the heart of the resort section in that state and winter sports attracts a great many tourests [sic], so I have desided [sic] to go up there and open a curio store. I am leaving tomorrow."[137]

The variegated shades of natural gray sheep's wool in this piece demonstrate a liveliness that was imparted to rugs with hand-carding and hand-spinning. The smooth and lustrous wool came from the Navajo Churro sheep. This breed's lineage can be traced back to the original sheep brought from Spain to the New World in the late sixteenth and early seventeenth centuries. The clean, long-staple fibers were well suited to Navajo hand-spinning. ALH

Navajo Rug

(Style influenced by Oriental carpets)

Likely exchanged or sold by the weaver to Crystal Trading Post,
Navajo Reservation, Crystal, New Mexico, late 19th–early 20th century
Hand-woven rug made with hand-carded and hand-spun native wool;
natural colors, synthetic red and black dyes
119.4 × 85.1 cm (47 × 33½ in.)
PROVENANCE: White Bear Rug Company, Highland Park, Illinois, 1998

The homespun and hand-woven qualities of an "artisanal" rug like this one would have appealed greatly to American collectors who sought to emphasize handwork and complement Craftsman-style furnishings in their homes. The simple color palette and bold patterns of this rug, intended as a floor covering, would have figured well into an interior scheme of the period. Navajo trader J. B. Moore understood this, placing advertisements for his Navajo wares in one of the Roycrofters' monthly Arts and Crafts magazines.[138]

Elements translated from Caucasian, Turkish, and other Middle Eastern rugs appear in many turn-of-the-century Navajo pieces. The central diamond and small hooked appendages (sometimes termed "latch hooks") derive from Oriental carpet designs that enterprising local traders showed to Navajo weavers in picture books or on linoleum tiles. The popular hooked motif occurs in more refined native textiles as well as in those of lesser quality. Exemplary hooked diamonds appear in J. B. Moore's 1911 sales catalog, along with a fancier version of this red and black reciprocating L border.[139]

The awkwardly woven shapes in this rug suggest the hand of a weaver with less control over her work — perhaps because she lacked experience or was beyond her prime. And although the white background may have appealed to certain buyers, as Clinton N. Cotton commented in 1896, "Lower priced [rugs] have generally considerable white in them."[140] In contrast, the skillfully and evenly carded gray wool indicates considerable expertise in spinning.

Despite the ungainly nature of the execution of some rugs, it is not true that Navajo weavers ever purposely integrated errors into their designs; this is a story transferred inappropriately from Oriental carpet lore to the American Southwest. Most Navajo weavers today attempt to correct any mistake of which they become aware. Many also acknowledge that to consider that a rug could be perfect, unless an error was intentionally added, is highly presumptuous. ALH

Made in 521—Green; 522—Brown; 523—Red; 524—Blue; 525—Delft Blue.

Made in 501—Green; 502—Brown; 503—Red; 504—Blue; 505—Delft Blue.

Made in 511—Green; 512—Brown; 513—Red; 514—Blue; 515—Delft Blue.

Sizes: 18″ x 36″; 24″ x 28″; 27″ x 54″; 30″ x 60″; 36″ x 72″; 54″ x 90″; 6′ x 9′; 6′ x 12′; 8′ x 10′; 8′ x 12′; 9′ x 12′; 9′ x 15′; 12′ x 15′.

Crex Grass Rugs of Minnesota

David Cathers

IN MARCH 1905, a Craftsman advertisement for the Craftsman Shops noted, "The approach of Spring brings with it the problem of Furnishings and Fittings for Country Homes, Seaside Cottages and Bungalows."[141] Among the Craftsman products said to solve this "problem" were "Grass Mattings and Rag Rugs."[142] That same month, Stickley's firm issued the catalog *Needle-Work from the Craftsman Workshops*. Included among its textile offerings was grass matting: "This is a heavy matting, soft-green in color — durable and adapted for use in any room."[143] While the maker of these rugs was not named in the catalog, it was most likely the American Grass Twine Company (AGT), the manufacturer of Crex grass rugs. Stickley sold these floor coverings either as matting — from 24 inches wide at $.30 a yard, to 120 inches wide at $1.75 a yard — or as fringed rugs, at slightly higher prices.

Foreign and domestic grass rugs had already begun showing up in *The Craftsman* before this advertisement was published. For instance, the floor of one bedroom of Craftsman House #11, published in November 1904, was "covered with a matting in a Japanese design introducing blues and greens."[144] In 1905 and 1906, Craftsman houses were often said to have "Japanese matting" or "green grass matting" on bedroom floors. An article on summertime furnishings in the May 1913 issue of *The Craftsman* suggested: "Rugs made of cool sea grass . . . woven . . . in Oriental countries." If Stickley bought Japanese matting to sell at retail, his most likely source was the vast Manhattan-based wholesaler and importer H. B. Claflin & Company.[145] A distributor of Crex rugs, Claflin probably supplied them to Stickley, though on at least one occasion the Craftsman Workshops bought Crex rugs directly from AGT.[146]

AGT came into existence in June 1899, a combination of the Northwestern Grass Twine Company — owner of the Wisconsin Grass Twine Plant of Oshkosh and the Minnesota Grass Twine Plant of St. Paul — and a new factory built in Superior, Wisconsin.[147] It was said to employ five hundred workers and boasted of plans to soon add a thousand more.[148] Its founding is a story that includes several familiar themes: American mechanical ingenuity and industrial production; the exploitation of natural resources; aggressive boosterism; and, eventually, the creation of a consumer product promoted by a consistent, sophisticated nationwide advertising campaign.

Besides its advertising in New York, Chicago, and Boston newspapers and in such magazines as *House Beautiful, Good Housekeeping, House & Garden, Harper's*

Bazaar made this point even more forcefully, linking modernity and hygiene. The copy urged readers to replace "old fashion [*sic*], woolen carpets, which collect dust and retain germs" with "CREX carpets . . . the ONLY Sanitary Floor Covering." A 1912 *House & Garden* advertisement said that the wire grass in Crex rugs "is a product of nature — unchanged and unharmed by any artificial process of manufacture." The firm's first advertisement in *The Craftsman*, in April 1909, called Crex rugs a "wonderful gift of nature. . . . From the Prairies of the West."[150] A hundred years later, these evocative advertisements read like twenty-first-century advertising for "natural" and "organic" consumer products, though in fact they spoke directly to early-twentieth-century fears of household dust and germs.

Crex advertising further promised that its rugs were affordable. A twenty-seven-inch-wide roll, for instance, sold at wholesale for $.28 per yard. In Stickley's 1905 catalog, this size was priced at $.31 per yard, a modest markup. A rug that was 10 × 144 inches wholesaled for $5.70; in lots of six, its unit price dropped to $5.40.[151] That size typically retailed for $7.50 to $7.95, though two Chicago department stores, Mandel Brothers and Schlesinger & Mayer, priced it at $8.00 and $8.25, respectively. When merchants held sales, however, the same rug was offered for as little as $6.50. That seems quite reasonable when compared to a Lanark Scotch Art Rug of 108 × 144 inches, on sale at Carson Pirie Scott for $15.00 in 1909, or a Scotch Art Rug of the same size offered for $27.50 that year by the Los Angeles merchant N. B. Blackstone. Crex rugs offered such a bargain because they became a favorite of big discounters; Macy's Manhattan department store, to cite one example, routinely advertised Crex rugs at "Lowest-in-the-city prices."[152]

The rugs were affordably priced and said to be easily cleaned; they therefore appealed to the modern, design-minded middle-class homemaker, whom Stickley saw as his market. These grass rugs were offered in at least one Craftsman catalog, sold in the Manhattan Craftsman Building and, for seven years, steadily advertised in *The Craftsman*. Crex rugs were appropriate Arts and Crafts floor coverings for Stickley's Craftsman houses.

ABOVE AND
OPPOSITE
Two pages from
Crex's 1916 catalog
showing the versatil-
ity of its grass rugs.
The Craftsman often
suggested Crex rugs
for bedrooms and
porches. Courtesy of
Cabincreekcds.com.

Bazaar, and *The Ladies' Home Journal*, Crex was a frequent *Craftsman* advertiser from 1909 through 1916. In the firm's consumer advertisements, Crex rugs were said to be artistic, economical, healthful, natural, and easy to keep clean. The firm's advertisement in the May 1907 issue of *House Beautiful*, for instance, extolled Crex rugs as "Nature's Carpet of Health. From the Fragrant Green Fields to Your Home."[149] The advertisement offered the assurance that "CREX is absolutely sanitary and will not retain germs and dust like heavy woolen carpets and rugs." The firm's advertisement in the June 1908 issue of *Harper's*

A CREX PORCH—TYPICAL OF THE HOMES OF THE MANY

Here is another CREX porch—not large or pretentious—but just like the porch of the average American home where the great majority of our people live. In every town there are hundreds of such porches, and in many cities can be seen thousands. A CREX rug of Rustic design (entirely new) with a CREX swing, chairs and table completes its modest and inexpensive furnishing, and yet who would say it is not comfortable and attractive?

Other green rugs are shown opposite—both plain and in figured designs. Select what you would like from our entire line shown in this catalog.

If your dealer cannot supply you write to us and we will let you know who can. This applies to CREX furniture as well.

Page Twenty-Six

Abnákee Rugs
of New Hampshire

David Cathers

IN HIS JULY 1901 *House Beautiful* review of the Providence Art Club's recent Arts and Crafts exhibition, the designer Theodore Hanford Pond praised only a handful of displays. He admired Grueby and Newcomb pottery, Tiffany Favrile glass, and "the Abnákee rugs by Miss Helen R. Albee . . . of Pequaket, New Hampshire."[153] An article in the June 1906 issue of *The Craftsman* spoke of "the famous Abnákee rugs, which the art sense and altruism of one woman have developed from the common 'hooked rug' of New England."[154] On August 8, 1909, the *Boston Daily Globe* called Albee a "creative genius."[155]

Another admirer of Abnákee rugs was Gustav Stickley. In 1902 an Abnákee rug was photographed in the Syracuse Craftsman Building, and the same rug apparently later figured among the original furnishings of Stickley's New Jersey home, Craftsman Farms.[156] The fact that an Abnákee rug appeared in a Stickley interior offers further proof of Albee's renown. However, perhaps because she worked in a delicate medium, little is known today about her output.[157]

Abnákee was a helpful mnemonic that echoed Albee's name. It also connected her rugs to the place where they were made — Pequaket, New Hampshire, an area once inhabited by a branch of the Eastern Abenaki, the Pequaket Indians. By bestowing this resonant brand name on her wares, Albee evoked poetic associations with the "authentic" Native Americans idealized by many Arts and Crafts supporters, who saw them as a people who lived simply, produced fine handicrafts, and existed in harmony with the natural world. Albee devised a distinctive logo and a silk label reading "The Abnákee Rug — Pequaket, N. H." and had it sewn onto the underside of her rugs. Perhaps the best contemporary account of Albee's work appeared in 1901:

OPPOSITE
Abnákee rug, 1897/1915.
Constructed of one-quarter-inch-wide wool flannel strips hand-hooked into a woven jute ground; 119.4 × 68.6 cm (47 × 27 in.). This design is similar to one illustrated in *The Craftsman,* June 1906, and often delineated in interiors in the magazine. Courtesy of the Wheeler family.

THIS PAGE
Albee's "lattice design with Indian border" rug at the entrance of the Lecture Hall in the Craftsman Building, Syracuse, New York, as illustrated in *The Craftsman,* December 1902.

The Abnákee rug . . . is the result of a desire on the part of Mrs. Helen R. Albee to give profitable employment to the women of the rural community where she lives. The thick, soft, velvety Abnákee rugs . . . are all wool, hand-dyed in warm tones of terra-cotta, old rose, old pink, tans, dull yellows, rich old blues, olive and sage greens, and old ivory. They are made to order usually, to match in

The 1903 Arts and Crafts First Annual Exhibition at the Art Institute of Chicago, December 1902–January 1903, with Albee's "lattice design with Indian border" rug hanging on the half wall at center. Courtesy of the Art Institute of Chicago, Archives Department.

OPPOSITE
An Abnákee rug designed by Helen Albee, 1897/1915; 106.7 × 68.6 cm (42 × 27 in.). By 1900 Albee had trained twenty women to produce Abnákee rugs. Albee bought wool exclusively from one mill and dyed it with proprietary aniline formulas to achieve her distinctive palette. Courtesy of the Wheeler family.

their ground color some special color in the room where they are to be placed, and the borders made in harmonious tones . . . the designs [are] original and distinctive.[158]

Helen Rickey (1864–1939) was born in Dayton, Ohio, and by about 1890 she was a student at the New York Institute for Artist-Artisans.[159] The school's educational methods stressed the "democratic conceptions of proportion, strength, harmony, grace, and beauty in combination with utility," thus adhering to Morris's famous dictum about the meshing of usefulness and beauty.[160] In accord with Arts and Crafts methods, students were taught to observe the natural world and derive motifs from plants and flowers, rather than imitate historic European styles. The institute was a forward-looking, handicraft-oriented establishment advocating "American art for American industry," and it was there that Albee learned design.[161]

Candace Wheeler was head of the institute's textile department. During the last quarter of the nineteenth century, Wheeler was the era's "acknowledged expert on all things having to do with decorative textiles and interiors."[162] A preeminent textile artist, she had, for a time, worked with Louis Comfort Tiffany as a partner in the interior design firm Associated Artists. She was also one of the first

career women, a role model for her students who encouraged women to take up craftwork as a path to artistic enrichment and economic self-sufficiency. As a teacher, artisan, and philanthropic businessperson, she was evidently an important influence for Albee. In an 1899 magazine article, Wheeler identified Albee as a former institute student who had established a hooked-rug industry. Taking obvious pride in her student's achievements, Wheeler wrote: "The change that has been wrought in this manufacture by an intelligent application of art is really marvelous. . . . The rugs . . . are a source of profitable labor to the community. I believe this to be the beginning of an important industry, which owes its success entirely to the art education of one woman."[163]

Albee had talent, training, and ambition. She had attended a school grounded in Arts and Crafts precepts, and one of her teachers was a successful businesswoman as well as the era's most notable textile authority. Within a few years of leaving the school, Albee had achieved a measure of varied professional success. In 1894 she married the writer John Albee, and that year they bought a summer home on a picturesque property in Pequaket, New Hampshire, a village within the country town of Tamworth, at the southern edge of the White Mountains. By 1898 they lived in Pequaket full time.[164]

Beginnings of the Abnákee Rug Industry

In Tamworth the Albees became part of the colony of wealthy urbanites — prosperous intellectual and artistic Bostonians — who vacationed there.[165] They also came into contact with the area's residents and witnessed the financial hardships faced by northern New Hampshire's dwindling populace. Farm families were increasingly abandoning the country for the city to find steady factory work, or seeking new lives in the American West. The plight of local farm wives — essentially uneducated, homebound, in need of money, and lacking marketable skills — attracted Albee's notice. Although she initially gave no thought to how she might assist them, her attitude changed. A magazine article later recounted the abrupt, initially frustrating awakening of her socially progressive idealism. A 1900 article in *Carpet and Upholstery Trade Review* reported: "The idea of helping [the farmwives] was suggested to her by Douglas Volk. 'We had been

talking ... about handicrafts and William Morris and John Ruskin in an artist's studio one afternoon, and ... Mr. Volk turned to me and asked: "What are you doing for those women in New Hampshire?" This question stayed with me, but when I put my services at their command they did not want any help.' "[166]

Albee was one of many educated, Progressive-era urban women who did good works among the underprivileged by promoting handicraft as a means of self-improvement.[167] As seems to have often been true of her reform-minded peers, she faced quite a culture shock.[168] Her middle-class attitudes were far removed from those of the provincial women she hoped to help, and there was unease on both sides of this socioeconomic gulf. She saw ugly hooked rugs on farmhouse floors and decided she could help the town's housewives make something better. They evidently did not feel the need to be "improved" by this well-to-do busybody from the city, and they resisted her efforts. Though well aware of the social and cultural implications of her work, and genuinely concerned with helping her neighbors "support their families and maintain their farms," Albee tended to view this class tension in largely aesthetic terms.[169] She wrote of her early experience in New Hampshire: "I was ... met with an impenetrable reserve.... My simple conventionalized designs had not met with their approval. I did not use bright colors; I wove no ... cats nor puppy dogs.... I had not reached the standards of native taste."[170]

Nevertheless, the farmwives knew how to make hooked rugs, albeit unaesthetic ones in Albee's view.[171] She was speaking of herself and others like her when she suggested that "competent women [should] undertake to turn this misdirected energy into some original and profitable channels."[172] By the time she wrote those words, she had already attracted several willing recruits. After starting her enterprise in about 1897, she could report definite, if qualified, progress by 1900: "They do not yet quite like my colors ... but I think they dislike them less than they did. During the three years since the industry began twenty women have been trained and 100 rugs have been made."[173] Like Stickley, Albee believed in strong management; she explained, "I saw daily the growing necessity of one person assuming full control."[174] Nonetheless, there can be no doubt of her altruism, and her fireside industry did benefit the community. A 1909 article about

Albee said, "In the rural districts, where profitable employment is not readily found, the craft has proved a blessing."[175]

Management and Business Practices

A 1904 report by the Bureau of Labor noted: "Mrs. Albee ... not only designs the patterns and cuts out stencils ... but also buys and dyes the flannel to be used for the filling, trains the workers, pays them for their work as it is finished, arranges for exhibits, takes orders, and markets the product."[176]

Her management style and no-nonsense view of Arts and Crafts were very like Stickley's. Both were at home in the world of commerce; both believed that machines had a legitimate place in craftwork; and both were occasionally criticized for not being ideologically "pure." They almost certainly knew each other: Albee wrote five articles for *The Craftsman*, and the magazine's coverage of Stickley's 1903 exhibition featured a photograph of an Abnákee rug.

Abnákee and Abnákee-like rugs were periodically visible in *The Craftsman*. In a November 1903 article by Harvey Ellis, an "Albee rug, with a body of subdued yellow and a border of cool tones of blue and green" was identified in an illustration. In June 1906, the magazine published a photograph of an Abnákee rug that it described as a "lattice design with Indian border" in green, red, orange, brown, and black.[177] That photograph appeared again in the November 1908 issue, and the following month, a drawing of a Craftsman house showed a living-room rug based on the Indian border design, though with no acknowledgment of Albee. An Abnákee rug of this design was also on the floor of Craftsman Farms by 1911, occupying a space between the Donegals in the dining room and the living-room druggets.

Stickley most likely bought that rug at the time of his 1903 exhibition, a date that suggests how much its harmonious colors and Native American–inspired design motifs aligned with the evolving Craftsman aesthetic. In March and April of that year, Native American rugs sent by Francis E. Lester adorned the walls of Stickley's Arts and Crafts exhibition. Woven Indian baskets, owned by the California writer George Wharton James, were also exhibited; their designs appealed to Stickley and, perhaps more important, captivated Harvey Ellis. When the exhibition traveled to Rochester, a local newspaper reporter wrote that he "found Harvey

OPPOSITE
Abnákee rug, 1897/1915, 142.2 × 94 cm (56 × 37 in.), signed "E. B." on the back. These are almost certainly the initials of Etta Bickford, whose name appears with Albee's in the catalog issued for the 1901 Providence, Rhode Island, Arts and Crafts exhibition. Albee encouraged craftswomen to draw their design inspiration from a variety of sources, including Oriental rugs. Courtesy of the Wheeler family.

Ellis in an attitude of adoration before a collection of Indian baskets."[178] By the end of May, of course, Ellis had moved to Syracuse and was working for Stickley. Among the many designs he contributed to *The Craftsman* that year were Native American–inspired graphics, wall stencils, and textiles.

Also in May 1903, Stickley opened the Craftsman textile and needlework department, directed by his employee Blanche Baxter. This department was soon adding new pattern, texture, and color to Craftsman interiors with embroidered and appliquéd table scarves, portières, and pillows covers, some based on Ellis's designs. By July, Ellis was enriching the largely brown and green-brown Craftsman color palette with yellow, turquoise, creamy white, and old rose; he was also instilling Craftsman architecture with vitality and sophistication and delineating the firm's first visually unified interior ensembles. In October he designed a Native American–inspired graphic for the magazine's cover, and in November George Wharton James wrote his first *Craftsman* article about Native American culture. By adapting Native American motifs and advocating domestic interiors that were unified by harmonious form and color, the Craftsman Workshops achieved an astonishing aesthetic feat, inventing its lush, new visual vocabulary in less than twelve months. With Stickley evidently playing the role of design director and chief motivator, this blossoming arose from the hand of Harvey Ellis and, in somewhat lesser roles, from Baxter, James, and Albee.

Like Morris, Voysey, and other Arts and Crafts rug designers, Albee created conventionalized natural forms and flat patterns. In her words, "Bold floral designs can be used if in flat colors . . . the flat form of flower or leaf . . . may have a beautiful outline if one is experienced in conventional design. . . . The suitability of a design to the purpose for which it is to be used is of great importance."[179]

Albee favored geometric forms. She used "simple elements such as squares, triangles, bars, [and] bands . . . decorative units built upon the straight line and angle."[180] And she developed definite ideas about how those generally rectilinear elements could best be deployed. As she wrote in *The Craftsman*, "The manner in which design is applied to any given area is of great importance. The simplest . . . way is to surround a plain center with a border made of repeated units. . . . A design may also be arranged with a plain ground and a border placed at either end. . . . If preferred, the plain ground of the rug may be broken by horizontal units placed at intervals."[181]

Albee said that her motifs were mostly drawn from Native American craftwork, though she acknowledged taking inspiration from Japanese, Persian, and Mexican decorative arts and from other "primitive" cultures. She also suggested studying Oriental rugs to learn "color and line effects," though she added firmly, "I do not advise imitating the designs."[182] Albee's stricture against copying Oriental rugs was meant to encourage originality, and it reflected the anti-historicist strand of the American movement. It was also sound business wisdom because, as she reminded her readers, "the market is full of [Oriental rugs] at all prices."[183]

Albee had many gifts. She was a designer, teacher, and artisan, and she was also an effective popularizer and a resourceful businesswoman. A master of flat pattern, harmonious color, and rich texture, she reinvented the prosaic hooked rug and elevated it to the level of artistic handicraft. Just as important, she was an idealist and philanthropist who brought the opportunity of meaningful work and modest income to her needy rural neighbors. Like Stickley, she was devoted to craft, and yet she also had a nondoctrinaire attitude toward machine-prepared materials, business management, and the demands of the American marketplace. For at least two decades, Albee was a significant and influential participant in the American Arts and Crafts movement, and her work, as Theodore Hanford Pond wrote in 1901, was indeed "most worthy of note."[184]

Endnotes

1 "Suitable Rugs for Craftsman Homes," *The Craftsman* 17, 6 (Feb. 1910), p. xxxviii.

2 "Mr. Stickley's 'Plea For A Democratic Art,'" *Carpet and Upholstery Trade Review* (hereafter C&UTR) 35 (Oct. 15, 1904), p. 111.

3 This phrase is often associated with Ralph Waldo Emerson, though he borrowed it from Wordsworth. In September 1904, it was used to describe one of the goals of *The Craftsman*: "It will continue, in the same strong terms as ever, to advocate plain living and high thinking." See "Notes," *The Craftsman* 6, 6 (Sept. 1904), p. 615.

4 The 1903 exhibition is discussed in detail in Irene Sargent, "A Recent Arts and Crafts Exhibition," *The Craftsman* 2, 4 (May 1903), pp. 69–73. See also Cathers 2003, pp. 72–79.

5 "Properly Appointed and Becoming Dwellings: Walls Floors and Woodwork as Harmonious Backgrounds," *The Craftsman* 27, 4 (Jan. 1915), p. 417.

6 *Chips from the Workshop of Gustave Stickley* (1901), n. pag.

7 "Good Domestic Rugs That Are within the Reach of People with Moderate Means," *The Craftsman* 17, 4 (Jan. 1910), p. 461.

8 "Craftsman Rugs Are Decorative as well as Useful and Harmonize Perfectly with the Furniture, Metal Work and Fabrics Used by the Craftsman in Home Furnishings and Decoration," *The Craftsman* 17, 1 (Oct. 1909), p. xliv.

9 The first head of the Craftsman textile and needlework department was Blanche R. Baxter (1870–1967); her responsibilities included providing her department with designs. She was later replaced by a member of her staff, Blanche L. Gildersleeve (active c. 1903–10), though it is not known if Gildersleeve also did design work. Victor Toothaker (1882–1932) is the only designer known to have been employed by Stickley from about 1907 to 1911, but he was mainly a metalworker, dividing his time between the metal shop and the office. There seems no way to know whether he designed Craftsman rugs.

10 *American Carpet and Upholstery Journal* 33 (June 1915), p. 37.

11 "Foreword," *The Craftsman* 1, 1 (Oct. 1901), n. pag.

12 "Foreword," *The Craftsman* 3, 1 (Oct. 1902), p. vii.

13 The author is very grateful to Diane Boucher for contributing text concerning Stickley and *The Craftsman* to this and later chapters. Morris used the term "Als ik Kan" in its German, French, and English translations, whereas Stickley used the modern Flemish form.

14 For a fuller survey of Morris's carpet production, see Parry 1983.

15 William Morris, "Textiles," a lecture to the Arts and Crafts Society, 1888.

16 In 1917 Morris & Co. moved its shop to George Street, Hanover Square.

17 Many machine-woven carpet techniques took their names from the area in Britain where they were first made during the eighteenth century. Simple machine-woven pile rugs are generally referred to as Wiltons and were first made by the Wilton Royal Carpet Manufactory in Wiltshire. Patent Axminster rugs, a type of pile carpet with a more complex pattern structure, were first made in Axminster in Devon. Kidderminster in Worcestershire was the home of flat-woven Kidderminsters; these were also known as Scotch carpets, as many were made in the Edinburgh and Glasgow areas of Scotland. These names led to great confusion in the nineteenth century, with different types being made all over Britain.

18 The Morris & Co. range also included Brussels carpeting, in which the pile is left uncut, providing a ridge or cord finish.

19 Arts and Crafts Exhibition Society, 1893, p. 37.

20 Arts and Crafts Exhibition Society, 1899, no. 277.

21 For more information about the Morris exhibitions in Boston, see Harvey and Press 1991, pp. 139–41.

22 The point paper for this carpet is illustrated in Barbara Morris, "William Morris, His Designs for Carpets and Tapestries," *Handweaver and Craftsman* (Fall 1961), p. 18.

23 Quoted in Parry 1983, p. 87.

24 From an estimate in the Victoria and Albert Museum (NAL.MS L.885-1954).

25 A number of these photographs are featured in Gleeson White, "An Epoch Making House," *The Studio* 12, 55 (1898), pp. 102–12.

26 Arts and Crafts Exhibition Society, 1899, no. 388.

27 Arts and Crafts Exhibition Society, 1889, no. 436.

28 Tattersall, 1934, p. 76.

29 Arts and Crafts Exhibition Society, 1889, no. 445.

30 Ibid., p. 184.

31 "Handicraft in Today's Civilization: A Survey of Conditions in Europe and America," *The Craftsman* 22, 3 (June 1912), p. 302. According to David Cathers, no corroborating evidence documenting this meeting between Stickley and Voysey exists.

32 Articles about Voysey, including those in *The Studio*, were available in North America by this date. His wallpaper and decorative designs were exhibited in major exhibitions, including the Chicago World's Columbian Exposition of 1893.00

33 In an article on the exhibition, Edward W. Gregory wrote: "Mr. Voysey occupies a position in decorative arts entirely to himself. He has had many followers and is unquestionably a designer of singular originality and power." See "The Seventh Exhibition of Arts and Crafts in London," *House & Garden* 3, 2 (Feb. 1903), pp. 208–13.

34 Arts and Crafts Exhibition Society, 1888, p. 5.

35 Crane, 1903.

36 Haslam, *Arts and Crafts*, 1991, p. 164.

37 Catalog of the Victorian and Edwardian Decorative Arts exhibition at the Victoria and Albert Museum (1952) ill. S29.

38 "Special Furniture Designed for Individual Homes: Illustrated by the Work of C. F. A. Voysey," *The Craftsman* 20, 5 (Aug. 1911), pp. 476–86.

39 Liberty & Co., *Irish Hand-Made Carpets* (1903), p. 11.

40 *The Studio* 8 (1896), p. 209.

41 *The Studio* 18 (1900), p. 47.

42 *Studio Yearbook* (1906), p. 71.

43 Liberty & Co. (1903), p. 8.

44 Alexander Millar, *The Art Journal* (1908), p. 22.

45 Unpublished handwritten notes by James Morton, private collection.

46 See Arts and Crafts Exhibition Society, 1899, cat. 261B, p. 91.

47 "Irish Carpet Exhibition," *The Furniture Record* (Mar. 1903).

48 Further color variations are illustrated in Haslam, *Arts and Crafts Carpets*, 1991, figs. 59 and 71; Haslam, "Vigour," 1991, no. 1; and Sherrill 1996, p. 300. An example in pinks and greens on a beige ground is now in the Victoria and Albert Museum. This was exhibited in the exhibition *Liberty 1875–1975* (D33).

49 See Haslam, *Arts and Crafts Carpets*, 1991, fig. 72.

50 "Als Ik Khan," *The Craftsman* 13, 4 (Jan. 1908), pp. 486–87.

51 "How the Government Could Aid in Bringing About a Much-Needed Reform in the Industrial System of This Country," *The Craftsman* 13, 5 (Feb. 1908), pp. 553–62.

52 For a fuller account of the Donegal development, see Larmour 1990–91.

53 Harold Rathbone founded the Della Robbia Pottery. See Harold Rathbone, "Report on the Second Exhibition of the Arts and Crafts Society in Dublin 1899," *Journal of the Proceedings of the Arts and Crafts Society of Ireland* 1, 3 (1901), p. 219.

54 Morton 1971, p. 94.

55 William Hunter, who was born in Scotland, represented Alexander Morton & Co. in the United States from 1889 until his death in 1905. The Englishman Herbert A. Witcombe later joined him during this period, and together they became the firm of Hunter and Witcombe. Following Hunter's death in 1905, George McGeachin, Morton's agent in Manchester, joined Witcombe in New York to form the partnership of Witcombe, McGeachin & Co. See "The New Firm of Witcombe, McGeachin & Co.," *C&UTR* 37 (Jan. 15, 1906), p. 92.

56 Arts and Crafts Exhibition Society, 1899, ill. 505.

57 "Suitable Rugs for Craftsman Homes," *The Craftsman* 17, 5 (Feb. 1910), p. xxxviii.

58 *C&UTR* 40 (Sept. 1909), p. 91.

59 "Open House," *The Craftsman* 10, 6 (Sept. 1906), p. xii.

60 Arts and Crafts Exhibition Society, 1899, no. 504.

61 Liberty & Co. (1903) no. 17.

62 Letter from Mary Watts to Donegal workers, 1899. Morton Papers, National Archive of Art and Design, Victoria and Albert Museum, London. Quoted in Haslam, *Arts and Crafts*, 1991, p. 128.

63 Letter from Mary Watts to Donegal workers, 1899. Morton Papers, National Archive of Art and Design, London. Quoted in Haslam, *Arts and Crafts Carpets*, 1991, p. 129.

64 See Morris 1989, p. 40; Haslam, *Arts and Crafts Carpets*, 1991, fig. 80; Haslam, "Vigour," 1991, no. 8.

65 See Larmour 1981; and Larmour 1990–91, p. 217.

66 Natalie Curtis, "The New Log House at Craftsman Farms: An Architectural Development of the Log Cabin," *The Craftsman* 21, 2 (Nov. 1911), pp. 196–203.

67 *Craftsman Furniture, Western Edition* (Apr. 1912), p. 52.

68 Quoted in Bowe and Cumming 1998, p. 114.

69 "The Dun Emer Industries in Ireland: A Successful Example of the Revival of Handicrafts in a Farming Community," *The Craftsman* 14, 1 (Apr. 1908), pp. 112–14.

70 Ibid.

71 Ibid.

72 Sherrill 1996, p. 306.

73 See also Haslam, *Arts and Crafts Carpets*, 1991, p. 186, fig. 139.

74 Bowe 1989, p. 197.

75 "The Rise of the Humble Rag Rug," *American Carpet and Upholstery Journal* 30 (Apr. 10, 1912), p. 56. Linda Parry also noted that the "colonial" prefix derives from the fact that the technique was brought to the United States from Britain with early eighteenth-century settlers, alongside quilting and other country crafts.

76 *Needle-Work from the Craftsman Workshops* (Mar. 1905), pp. 59–61.

77 C&UTR 38 (Jan. 15, 1907), p. 91.

78 See, for instance, Gustav Stickley, "Furniture Based upon Good Craftsmanship," *The Craftsman* 29, 5 (Feb. 1916), pp. 531–38; and Mary Fanton Roberts, "One Man's Story," *The Craftsman* 30, 2 (May 1916), pp. 188–200.

79 Von Rosenstiel, 1978, pp. 27–30.

80 Kidderminster and ingrain are the names of a type of rug; Kidderminster is also the name of an English city that was a center for weaving. Ingrain is a plain-weave fabric of two- or three-ply woolen weft on a cotton warp. The making of ingrain rugs began in Kidderminster in the eighteenth century. For United States production of ingrain carpets, see Faraday 1929, p. 352. For a brief discussion of these alternate names, see Sherrill 1996, p. 215. For definitions, see Von Rosenstiel 1978, pp. 181–82.

81 *The Craftsman* 17, 2 (Nov. 1909), p. xliv.

82 Unpublished handwritten notes by James Morton, private collection.

83 Holt 1901, p. 24.

84 "India Carpets," C&UTR 30 (Aug. 15, 1899), p. 49; and "A Great Assortment of Rugs," C&UTR 30 (Oct. 15, 1899), pp. 53–54.

85 C&UTR 31 (Aug. 15, 1900), pp. 52, 101.

86 C&UTR 32 (June 15, 1901), p. 48.

87 C&UTR 32 (June 1, 1901), p. 125.

88 "A Notable Report on India Rugs," C&UTR 37 (Nov. 15, 1906), p. 90. Sloane was still importing rugs from India when it advertised in *The Craftsman* 25, 3 (Dec. 1913), p. 2a.

89 "Carpets and Rugs From the Orient: The H. B. Claflin Company," C&UTR 35 (July 1, 1902), p. 35.

90 Oliver Coleman, "Notes and Comments," *House Beautiful* 13, 3 (Feb. 1903), pp. 193–194.

91 *The Craftsman* 23, 5 (Feb. 1913), p. 23a.

92 "Craftsman Furnishings for the Ordinary Room," *The Craftsman* 21, 1 (Oct. 1911), pp. 105–09.

93 Ibid.

94 "Craftsman House No. VII, Series 1904," *The Craftsman*, 6, 4 (July 1904), p. 401.

95 *Needle-Work from the Craftsman Workshops* (Mar. 1905), pp. 62–63.

96 Sherrill 1996, p. 347.

97 Ibid., p. 344.

98 Ibid., pp. 344–47.

99 *American Carpet and Upholstery Journal* 30 (Feb. 10, 1912), p. 45.

100 Ibid.

101 Sherrill 1996, p. 147.

102 *Needle-Work from the Craftsman Workshops*, (Mar. 1905), p. 59.

103 "Distinction and Charm Given to the Ordinary Room by Craftsman Furniture," *The Craftsman* 21, 1 (Oct. 1911), pp. 106–09.

104 *Needle-Work from the Craftsman Workshops*, (Mar. 1905), p. 59.

105 Sherrill 1996, p. 147.

106 *Craftsman Furniture Made by Gustav Stickley at the Craftsman Workshops*, Eastern Edition, (July 1910), p. 123.

107 "Craftsman Furnishing for the Ordinary Room," *The Craftsman* 21, 1 (Oct. 1911), p. 109.

108 *Craftsman Furnishings for the Home*, Western Edition (Apr. 1912), p. 53.

109 George De Szögyénÿ, "Profitable Handicrafts and the Successful Promotion of Home Industries," *The Craftsman* 13, 6 (Mar. 1908), pp. 653–62.

110 There was a widespread belief, equated with a theory of biological evolution, that the so-called primitive societies were still at the beginning of human civilization, while the white man of modern Europe and the United States was at the top level. This was a wholly unproven theory. The pioneering anthropologist Franz Boas (1858–1942) finally repudiated the notion of a cultural evolution in his book *Primitive Art*, published in 1927. The book was based on his extensive study of the art of the Native American tribes of the Pacific Northwest. See Gombrich 2002 for a detailed discussion on this topic.

111 Giles Edgerton, "Is America Selling Her Birthright in Art for a Mess of Pottage? Significance of This Year's Exhibit at the Pennsylvania Academy," *The Craftsman* 11, 6 (Mar. 1907), p. 658.

112 "Nursery Wall Coverings in Indian Designs," *The Craftsman* 5, 1 (Oct. 1903), pp. 95–99.

113 Ibid.

114 "Indian Blankets, Baskets, and Bowls: The Product of the Original Craftworkers of this Continent," *The Craftsman* 17, 5 (Feb. 1910), pp. 588–90.

115 Frederick Monsen, "The Destruction of Our Indians: What Civilization Is Doing to Extinguish an Ancient and Highly Intelligent Race by Taking Away Its Arts, Industries and Religion," *The Craftsman* 11, 4 (Mar. 1907), pp. 683–91.

116 Ibid.

117 Charles Frederick Holder, "Some Queer Laborers—Where Peaceful Living Is Preferred to Money Making," *The Craftsman* 10, 6 (Sept. 1906), pp. 752–60.

118 The Francis E. Lester Company was a frequent advertiser in *The Craftsman* beginning in 1903. In February 1904, the firm acquired the American-Mexican Importing Company of San Antonio, Texas. The list of Indian goods in its 1904 catalog included war clubs, arrowheads, baskets, beadwork, dance rattles, tom-toms, and rugs made by the Pueblo and Navajo peoples, as well as Mexican handmade lace and rugs. See *The Craftsman* 21, 4 (Jan. 1912), p. 22a.

119 *The Craftsman* 23, 6 (Mar. 1913), p. 7a.

120 "The American Santa Claus and His Gifts," *The Craftsman* 27, 3 (Dec. 1914), pp. 338–43.

121 "Three 'Craftsman Canvas' Pillows," *The Craftsman* 5, 1 (Oct. 1903), p. 94.

122 "Nursery Wall Coverings in Indian Designs," *The Craftsman* 5, 1 (Oct. 1903), p. 95.

123 "Correspondence," *The Craftsman* 5, 3 (Dec. 1903), p. 317.

124 "Porches, Pergolas and Balconies, and the Charm of Privacy Out of Doors," *The Craftsman* 9, 6 (Mar. 1906), pp. 843–45.

125 "The Craftsman Bungalow, Open Door," *The Craftsman* 7, 6 (Mar. 1905), p. 756.

126 "A Craftsman Bungalow: Craftsman House Series of 1905, #3," *The Craftsman* 7, 6 (Mar. 1905), p. 739.

127 Charles A. Eastman (Ohiyesa), "My People: The Indians' Contribution to the Art of America," *The Craftsman* 27, 2 (Nov. 1914), pp. 179–86.

128 Robert S. Phillips, "'Illahee,' A Sample of What the Northwest Is Doing in Architecture and Gardening," *The Craftsman* 31, 1 (Oct. 1916), p. 72.

129 Williams 1989, p. 63.

130 Baer, 1987, p. 76.

131 Moore 1911, p. 10. in J. B. Moore, *The Catalogues of Fine Navajo Blankets, Rugs, Ceremonial Baskets, Silverware, Jewelry & Curious* [1903–1911], reprinted by Avanyu Publishing (1987), Albuquerque, NM.

132 Adeline P. Alcutt to Hubbell Trading Post, Ganado, Arizona, Dec. 31, 1902. Hubbell Trading Post Records, Box 86, Wigwam Folder.

133 Adeline P. Alcutt to Hubbell Trading Post, Ganado, Arizona, Feb. 1, 1903. Hubbell Trading Post Records, Box 86, Wigwam Folder.

134 Adeline P. Alcutt to Hubbell Trading Post, Ganado, Arizona, Dec. 1, 1902. Hubbell Trading Post Records, Box 86, Wigwam Folder.

135 R. N. Stites to Hubbell Trading Post, Ganado, Arizona, Dec. 1904. Hubbell Trading Post Records, Box 78, Stites Folder.

136 R. N. Stites to Hubbell Trading Post, Ganado, Arizona, July 1905. Hubbell Trading Post Records, Box 78, Stites Folder.

137 W. S. Wilber to Hubbell Trading Post, Ganado, Arizona, Oct. 9, 1940. Hubbell Trading Post Records, Box 86, Wilber Folder.

138 Wilkins 2008, p. 65.

139 Moore 1911, pls. XVI, XXIII and XXV.

140 Quoted in Williams 1989, p. 63.

141 *The Craftsman*, 7, 6 (Mar. 1906) p. xxx.

142 Ibid.

143 *Needle-Work from the Craftsman Workshops* (Mar. 1905), p. 63.

144 "Craftsman House, Series of 1904, #11," *The Craftsman* 7, 2 (Nov. 1904), pp. 208–21.

145 Gustav Stickley, Business Papers, Winterthur Library.

146 *C&UTR* 32 (July 1, 1901), p. 61; "Grass Matting: H. B. Claflin Co.," *C&UTR* 32 (Oct. 1, 1901), p. 19.

147 "American Grass Twine Company Incorporated," *New York Times*, June 8, 1899, p. 5. For the firm's 1908 name change to the Crex Carpet Company, see "American Grass Twine Company to Reorganize," *C&UTR* 39 (Sept. 15, 1908), p. 78.

148 "Plans of Grass Twine Trust," *New York Times*, June 20, 1899, p. 7.

149 Advertisement for Crex Carpet Company, *House Beautiful* (May 1907).

150 Advertisement for Crex Carpet Company, *The Craftsman* 16, 1 (Apr. 1909), p. xxv.

151 "Revised Price List: Crex Matting, Art Squares and Rugs," *C&UTR* 37 (Feb. 15, 1906), p. 120.

152 For Mandel Brothers, see *Chicago Daily Tribune*, Apr. 30, 1908, p. 6; for Schlesinger & Mayer, see *Chicago Daily Tribune*, May 25, 1903, p. 5; for Carson Pirie Scott, see *Chicago Daily Tribune*, Sept. 1, 1909, p. 22; for N. B. Blackstone, see *Los Angeles Times*, Oct. 17, 1909, p. III4; for Macy's, see *New York Times*, June 27, 1915, p. S1.

153 Theodore Hanford Pond, "The Arts and Crafts Exhibition at the Providence Art Club," *House Beautiful* 10 (June 1901), pp. 98–101.

154 "Distinctive American Rugs: Designed and Woven in the Homes of Country Women," *The Craftsman* 10, 3 (June 1906), pp. 366–77.

155 "Abnákee Rug Making," *Boston Daily Globe*, Aug. 8, 1909, p. SM 5.

156 For Craftsman Farms, see www.stickleymuseum.org.

157 For more on Albee, see Richardson 2001.

158 Holt 1901, pp. 110–11.

159 Helen Rickey's name does not appear in any of the Manhattan or Brooklyn city directories from 1888 to 1894, and it has not been possible to determine the exact dates of her enrollment at the institute.

160 "Art Wedded to Industry," *New York Times*, Mar. 17, 1889, p. 2.

161 Ibid.

162 Peck and Irish 2001, p. 3.

163 Candace Wheeler, "Home Industries and Domestic Manufactures," *The Outlook* 63 (Oct. 14, 1899), pp. 402–06.

164 Richardson 2001, pp. 86, 88.

165 Much of this paragraph is based on Albee's writings and on Richardson's essay. It also draws on Garvin 2001; and Austen 2001.

166 "Drawn Rag Rugs," C&UTR 31 (June 1, 1900), pp. 51–52. Douglas Volk was a painter and teacher. He and his wife, Marion, lived in New York City and summered at their home in Center Lovell, Maine.

167 This subject is discussed in detail in Gordon 1998.

168 This subject is discussed at length in Whisnant 1983, pp. 19–101. A good survey of New England rug making may be found in the chapter "Handmade Rugs and Carpets," in Eaton 1949, pp. 113–31.

169 Garvin 2001, p. 72.

170 Albee 1901, pp. 15–16.

171 Rug hooking involves pulling strips of cloth or yarn through the interstices of a mesh burlap foundation to form a surface composed of loops; like other hooked-rug makers, Albee sheared some of the loops to enliven surface texture.

172 Helen R. Albee, "A Profitable Philanthropy," *The American Monthly Review of Reviews* 22 (July 1900), pp. 57–60.

173 "Drawn Rag Rugs," C&UTR 31 (June 1, 1900), pp. 51–52.

174 Albee 1901, p. 19.

175 "Abnákee Rug Making," *Boston Daily Globe*, Aug. 8, 1909, p. SM 5.

176 West, 1904, p. 1587.

177 An Abnákee rug, apparently another example of this design, had earlier appeared in Helen R. Albee, "Making Successful Rugs in Country Homes," *Country Life in America* 8 (Aug. 1905), p. 412. See Helen R. Albee, "Developing a Home Industry: How the Abnákee Rug Grew Out of the Old Fashioned Hooked Mat of Our Grandmothers," *The Craftsman* 15, 2 (Nov. 1908), pp. 236–41.

178 "Arts and Crafts 'Hanging Day,'" *Rochester Post*, Apr. 13, 1903.

179 Albee 1901, p. 34.

180 Helen R. Albee, "Developing a Home Industry: How the Abnákee Rug Grew Out of the Old-Fashioned Hooked Mat of Our Grand-Mothers," *The Craftsman* 15, 2 (Nov. 1908), pp. 236–41.

181 Ibid., p. 24.

182 Albee 1901, p. 34.

183 Ibid.

184 Theodore Hanford Pond, "The Arts and Crafts Exhibition at the Providence Art Club," *House Beautiful* 10 (June 1901), pp. 98–100.

Selected Bibliography

Albee, Helen R. 1901. *Abnákee Rugs.* Riverside Press.

Arts and Crafts Exhibition Society. 1893. *Arts and Crafts Essays.* Rivington, Percival, and Co.

———. 1888. *Catalogue of the First Exhibition.* Exh. cat. New Gallery.

———. 1889. *Catalogue of the Second Exhibition.* Exh. cat. New Gallery.

———. 1899. *Catalogue of the Sixth Exhibition.* Exh. cat. New Gallery.

Arts and Crafts Society of Ireland. 1896. *Journal of the Proceedings of the Arts and Crafts Society of Ireland.* Arts and Crafts Society of Ireland.

Austen, Barbara. 2001. "'For the Sake of Others': The Role of Women in the New Hampshire Crafts Revival, 1897–1931." *Historical New Hampshire* 56 (Fall/Winter), pp. 68–85.

Ayres, Dianne, et al. 2002. *American Arts and Crafts Textiles.* Harry N. Abrams.

Baer, Elizabeth. 1987. "Research for a Catalog of the Navajo Textiles of Hubbell Trading Post." Report for National Endowment for the Humanities Grant No. GM-22317-85.

Blomberg, Nancy J. 1988. *Navajo Textiles: The William Randolph Hearst Collection.* University of Arizona Press.

Bowe, Nicola Gordon. 1989. "Two Early Twentieth-Century Irish Arts and Crafts Workshops in Context: An Túr Gloine and the Dun Emer Guild and Industries." *Journal of Design History* 2, 2–3, pp. 193–206.

———. 1996. "The Search for Vernacular Expression: The Arts and Crafts Movement in America and Ireland." In *The Substance of Style: Perspectives on the American Arts and Crafts Movement,* edited by Bert Denker, pp. 5–24. Henry Francis du Pont Winterthur Museum/University Press of New England.

Bowe, Nicola Gordon, and Elizabeth Cumming. 1998. *The Arts and Crafts Movement in Dublin and Edinburgh: 1885–1925.* Irish Academic Press.

Callen, Anthea. 1979. *Women Artists of the Arts and Crafts Movement: 1870–1914.* Pantheon Books.

Cathers, David M. 2003. *Gustav Stickley.* Phaidon.

Caw, James L. 1900. "The Mortons of Darvel." *Art Journal* (Jan.), pp. 78–82.

Cole, Arthur Harrison, and Harold Francis Williamson. 1941. *The American Carpet Manufacture: A History and an Analysis.* Harvard University Press.

Crane, Walter. 1903. *Catalogue of the Seventh Exhibition.* Exh. cat. Chiswick Press.

Dresser, Christopher. 1995. *Principles of Victorian Decorative Design.* 1873. Repr., Dover Publications.

Durant, Stuart. 1992. *CFA Voysey.* Architectural Monographs 19. Academy Editions/St. Martin's Press.

Eaton, Allen H. 1949. *Handicrafts of New England.* Harper and Brothers Publishers.

Fairclough, Oliver, and Emmeline Leary. 1981. *Textiles by William Morris and Morris and Co., 1861–1940.* Thames and Hudson/Eastview Editions.

Faraday, Cornelia Bateman. 1929. *European and American Carpets and Rugs.* Dean-Hicks Company.

Foster, R. F. 1997. *W. B. Yeats: A Life. I. The Apprentice Mage, 1865–1914.* Oxford University Press.

Garvin, Donna-Belle. 2001. "'Back to Nature': Summer Communities and the Craft Revival in New Hampshire — An Introduction." *Historical New Hampshire* 56 (Fall/Winter), pp. 68–73.

Gebhard, David. 1971. "C. F. A. Voysey: To and From America." *Journal of the Society of Architectural Historians* 30, 4 (Dec.), pp. 304–12.

Gombrich, E. H. 2002. *The Preference for the Primitive: Episodes in the History of Western Taste and Art.* Phaidon.

Gordon, Beverly. 1998. "Spinning Wheels, Samplers, and the Modern Priscilla: The Images and Paradoxes of Colonial Revival Needlework." *Winterthur Portfolio* 33 (Summer/Autumn), pp. 163–94.

Harvey, Charles, and Jon Press. 1991. *William Morris, Design and Enterprise in Victorian England.* Manchester University Press/St. Martin's Press.

Haslam, Malcolm. 1991. *Arts and Crafts Carpets.* David Black.

———. 1991. "Vigour of the Outer Air." *Hali* 57 (June), pp. 107–13.

Hedlund, Ann Lane. 1997. *Navajo Weavings from the Andy Williams Collection.* Exh. cat. Saint Louis Art Museum.

———. 2004. *Navajo Weaving in the Late Twentieth Century: Kin, Community, and Collectors.* University of Arizona Press.

Herzog, Melanie. 1996. "Aesthetics and Meanings: The Arts and Crafts Movement and the Revival of American Indian Basketry." In *The Substance of Style: Perspectives on the American Arts and Crafts Movement,* edited by Bert Denker, pp. 69–91. Henry Francis du Pont Winterthur Museum/University Press of New England.

Hewitt, Mark A. 2001. *Gustav Stickley's Craftsman Farms: The Quest for an Arts and Crafts Utopia.* Syracuse University Press.

Hicks, Ami Mali. 1936. *The Craft of Hand-Made Rugs.* Empire State Book Co.

Holt, Rosa Belle. 1901. *Rugs, Oriental and Occidental, Antique and Modern: A Handbook for Ready Reference.* A. C. McClurg and Co.

Hubbell Trading Post, 1882–1968. Hubbell Trading Post Records, AZ 375, University of Arizona Library Special Collection, Tucson.

Hunterian Art Gallery. 1986. *Art Nouveau Designs from the Silver Studio Collection, 1885–1910.* Middlesex Polytechnic.

James, George Wharton. 1974. *Indian Blankets and Their Makers.* 1920. Repr., Dover Publications.

Kahlenberg, Mary Hunt, and Anthony Berlant. 1972. *The Navajo Blanket.* Exh. cat. Praeger.

Kaplan, Wendy. 2004. "America: A Quest for Democratic Design." In *The Arts and Crafts Movement in Europe and America: Design for the Modern World*, pp. 264–283. Exh. cat. Thames and Hudson/Los Angeles County Museum.

Kaplan, Wendy, and Eileen Boris. 1987. *"The Art That Is Life": The Arts and Crafts Movement in America, 1875–1920*. Exh. cat. Little, Brown.

Kaufman, Alice, and Christopher Selser. 1985. *The Navajo Weaving Tradition: 1650 to the Present*. Dutton.

Kirk, Sheila. 2005. *Philip Webb: Pioneer of Arts and Crafts Architecture*. Wiley-Academy.

Larmour, Paul. 1981. *Celtic Ornament*. The Irish Heritage Series 33. Eason and Son.

————. 1984. "The Dun Emer Guild." *Irish Arts Review* 1, 4 (Winter), pp. 24–28.

————. 1990–91. "Donegal Carpets." *Irish Arts Review Yearbook*, pp. 210–16.

————. 1992. *The Arts and Crafts Movement in Ireland*. Friar's Bush Press.

Lemos, Pedro J., et al. 1920. *Applied Art: Drawing, Painting, Design, and Handicraft*. Pacific Press Pub. Association.

Liberty & Co. 1903. *Irish Hand-Made Carpets*. Exh. cat. Liberty & Co.

————. 1907. *Founding a National Industry: A Special Collection and Exhibition of the New Irish Hand-Made Carpets*. Exh. cat. Liberty & Co.

Livingstone, Karen, and Linda Parry, eds. 2005. *International Arts and Crafts*. Exh. cat. Victoria and Albert Museum/Harry N. Abrams.

Lynn, Catherine. 1986. "Surface Ornaments: Wallpapers, Carpets, Textiles, and Embroidery." In Doreen Bolger, *In Pursuit of Beauty: Americans and the Aesthetic Movement*. Exh. cat. Rizzoli/Metropolitan Museum of Art.

MacKail, J. W. 1995. *The Life of William Morris*. 1899. Repr., Dover Publications.

Martin, Stephen A., ed. 2001. *Archibald Knox*. Artmedia.

McCorquodale, Charles. 1983. *The History of Interior Decoration*. Phaidon.

M'Closkey, Kathy. 2002. *Swept under the Rug: A Hidden History of Navajo Weaving*. University of New Mexico Press.

McManis, Kent, et al. 1997. *A Guide to Navajo Weavings*. Treasure Chest Books.

McNitt, Frank. 1962. *The Indian Traders*. University of Oklahoma Press.

Moore, John B. 1987. *The Catalogues of Fine Navajo Blankets, Rugs, Ceremonial Baskets, Silverware, Jewelry, and Curios*. 1903–11. Repr., Avanyu Publishing.

Morris, Barbara J. 1989. *Liberty Design, 1874–1914*. Chartwell Books.

————. 1998. "Liberty's Pioneer Designer." In *Mary Seton Watts (1849–1938): Unsung Heroine of the Art Nouveau*, edited by Veronica Franklin Gould, pp. 11–14. Exh. cat. Watts Gallery.

Morton, James. 1867–1943. Unpublished diary.

Morton, Jocelyn. 1971. *Three Generations in a Family Textile Firm*. Routledge and Kegan Paul.

————. 1973. *The Mortons: Three Generations of Textile Creation*. Exh. cat. Victoria and Albert Museum.

Murphy, William S. 1910. *The Textile Industries: A Practical Guide to Fibres, Yarns, and Fabrics*. 6 vols. Gresham Pub. Co.

Myrick, Herbert. 1901. *Creating New Industries*. Orange Judd Co.

Parry, Linda. 1983. *William Morris Textiles*. Weidenfeld and Nicolson.

————, ed. 1996. *William Morris*. Exh. cat. Philip Wilson/Victoria and Albert Museum.

————. 2005. *Textiles of the Arts and Crafts Movement*. 1988. Repr., Thames and Hudson.

Peck, Amelia, and Carol Irish. 2001. *Candace Wheeler: The Art and Enterprise of American Design, 1875–1900*. Exh. cat. Metropolitan Museum of Art/Yale University Press.

Richardson, Cynthia Watkins. 2001. "'A Profitable Philanthropy': The Abnákee Rug Industry of Helen Albee of Tamworth." *Historical New Hampshire* 56 (Fall/Winter), pp. 86–103.

Rodee, Marian E. 1981. *Old Navajo Rugs: Their Development from 1900 to 1940*. University of New Mexico Press.

————. 1995. *One Hundred Years of Navajo Rugs*. University of New Mexico Press.

Ruskin, John. 2003. *The Stones of Venice*. Edited by J. G. Links. 1960. Repr., Da Capo Press.

Sheehy, Jeanne. 1980. *The Rediscovery of Ireland's Past: The Celtic Revival, 1830–1930*. Thames and Hudson.

Sherrill, Sarah B. 1996. *Carpets and Rugs of Europe and America*. Abbeville Press.

Simpson, Duncan. 1979. *C. F. A. Voysey: An Architect of Individuality*. Lund Humphries.

Stickley, Gustav. 1989. *The Collected Works of Gustav Stickley*. Edited by Stephen Gray and Robert Edwards. 1981. Repr., Turn of the Century Editions.

Stubblebine, Ray. 2006. *Stickley's Craftsman Homes: Plans, Drawings, Photographs*. Gibbs Smith.

Tattersall, C. E. C. 1934. *A History of British Carpets*. F. Lewis.

Teehan, Virginia, and Elizabeth Wincott Heckett, eds. 2004. *The Honan Chapel*. Cork University Press.

Tilbrook, Adrian J. 1995. *The Designs of Archibald Knox for Liberty and Co.* 2nd ed. Richard Dennis.

Todd, Mattie Phipps. 1902. *Hand-Loom Weaving: A Manual for School and Home*. Rand, McNally and Company.

Tomes, Nancy. 1998. *The Gospel of Germs: Men, Women, and the Microbe in American Life*. Harvard University Press.

Vallance, Aymer. 1897. *William Morris: His Art, His Writings, and His Public Life*. G. Bell.

Victoria and Albert Museum. 1952. *Victorian and Edwardian Decorative Arts*. Exh. cat. H. M. Stationery Office.

Von Rosenstiel, Helene. 1978. *American Rugs and Carpets from the Seventeenth Century to Modern Times*. Morrow.

Voysey correspondence and archives, 1875–1941. National Art Library and Royal Institute of British Architects, Victoria and Albert Museum, London.

Walker, Lydia Le Baron. 1929. *Homecraft Rugs*. Frederick A. Stokes Company.

West, Max. 1904. *The Revival of Handicrafts in America*. Bulletin of the Bureau of Labor.

Wheat, Joe Ben, and Anne Lane Hedlund. 2003. *Blanket Weaving in the Southwest*. University of Arizona Press.

Whisnant, David E. 1983. *"All That Is Native and Fine": The Politics of Culture in an American Region*. University of North Carolina Press.

Wilkins, Teresa. 2008. *Patterns of Exchange: Navajo Weavers and Traders*. University of Oklahoma Press.

Williams, Lester L. 1989. *C. N. Cotton and His Navajo Blankets*. Avanyu Publishing.

Stickley Catalogs and Booklets

1901

Chips from the Workshops of Gustave Stickley

Chips from the Workshops of the United Crafts

Things Wrought by the United Crafts

1902

Things Wrought by the United Crafts for Marshall Field & Co, Chicago

1904

What Is Wrought in the Craftsman Workshops

1905

Craftsman Furnishings

Needle-Work from the Craftsman Workshops

The Craftsman's Story

1906

Chips from the Craftsman Workshops Number II

Craftsman Furnishings

1907

Chips from the Craftsman Workshops

1908

Craftsman Fabrics and Needlework

1909

Craftsman Furniture Made by Gustav Stickley at the Craftsman Workshops

Some Chips from the Craftsman Workshops

1910

Craftsman Furniture Made by Gustav Stickley at the Craftsman Workshops, Eastern Edition

Craftsman Furniture Made by Gustav Stickley at the Craftsman Workshops, Western Edition

1912

Craftsman Furnishings for the Home

Craftsman Furniture, Eastern Edition

Craftsman Furniture, Western Edition

1913

Craftsman Furniture

1915

Craftsman Department of Interior Furnishings

Selected Periodicals

American Carpet and Upholstery Journal (1883–1942)

The American Monthly Review of Reviews (1897–1907)

Carpet and Upholstery Trade Review (1889–36)

The Craftsman (1901–16)

House Beautiful (1896–1910)

The Studio (1893–1964)

Studio Yearbook (1906–1926)

The Outlook (1893–1928)

About the Authors

Linda Parry is a freelance writer and curator. For over thirty years, she was a curator in the textile department at the Victoria and Albert Museum in London. Her books include *William Morris Textiles* (1983), *Textiles of the Arts and Crafts Movement* (1988), and *William Morris* (1996). She also organized the major museum exhibitions *Textiles of the Arts and Crafts Movement* (1988) and William Morris (1996) and was a coeditor of the publication *International Arts and Crafts* (2005), which accompanied an exhibition of the same name. She is a Fellow of the Society of Antiquaries of London and was awarded an MBE in the Queen's Honours List for 2006.

David Cathers is a writer and museum consultant whose published works include *Furniture of the American Arts and Crafts Movement* (1981, 1996), *Stickley Style* (1999), and *Gustav Stickley* (2003). He was the 2005 recipient of the Stickley Museum at Craftsman Farms' *Als Ik Kan* Award.

Diane Boucher, an art historian, has done extensive research on the Crab Tree Farm Collection and has published articles on the subject in *Style 1900* (2009) and *Hali* (2009).

Ann Lane Hedlund directs the Gloria F. Ross Tapestry Program at the Arizona State Museum, University of Arizona, Tucson, where she is also a curator of ethnology and professor of anthropology at the university. Hedlund edited Joe Ben Wheat's award-winning book *Blanket Weaving in the Southwest* (2003). Her book, *Navajo Weaving in the Late Twentieth Century: Kin, Community, and Collectors* (2004), won the Arizona Highways/Arizona Library Association Award for Nonfiction in 2005.

Dru Muskovin has worked at Crab Tree Farm for nineteen years. Her primary work is in textile restoration and conservation of the collection, including the use of period fabrics in room settings. She has also worked on the creation of reproductions and historically accurate interpretations of Craftsman textiles.

Drawing of the interior of a Craftsman living room published in *The Craftsman*, October 1905.

Acknowledgments

The concept of examining Arts and Crafts rugs through the lens of *The Craftsman* magazine came from Dru Muskovin. For close to twenty years, Dru has been responsible for the care and conservation of the textile collections at Crab Tree Farm. Without her this book would not have been realized.

Unlike Arts and Crafts furniture, ceramics, metalware, and textiles, the rugs have not been the subject of thorough examination. We are indebted to Linda Parry, David Cathers, Diane Boucher, and Ann Lane Hedlund for their pioneering research and insightful observations.

Many people generously shared their knowledge and rugs with us or helped with research and logistics, making the book a far more textured study. In particular we thank Jack Brown and the reference staff at the Ryerson and Burnham Libraries, Art Institute of Chicago; Bob Cottrell, director of the Remick Country Doctor Museum and Farm, Tamworth, New Hampshire; Martin Levy of H. Blairman & Sons, London; Crex Meadow Wildlife Area, Grantsburg, Wisconsin; Cornelia W. Lanou; the reference staff at New Mexico State University, Las Cruces, New Mexico; Mrs. John Brandon-Jones; Arto and Eddy Keshishian of Antique Carpets, Tapestries and Aubussons, London; Michael McCracken; Jeanne Solensky of the Winterthur Museum, Garden, and Library, Winterthur, Delaware; and David A. Taylor.

Kim Coventry was responsible for managing the project and editing the text. Tom Gleason and Marcia Kronenberg provided valuable assistance throughout the process. Jamie Stukenberg took the majority of the photographs of the room interiors and the rugs themselves. Hal Kugeler wove all these elements into a sensitive and compelling design.

Finally, I thank Nancy Green, senior editor at W. W. Norton, for her enthusiasm and willingness to usher this book into publication.

John H. Bryan
Crab Tree Farm

OPPOSITE
Woman's bedroom in the Crab Tree Cottage at Crab Tree Farm, with a hand-knotted rug drawn in the Morton Studio and probably based on designs by Archibald Knox or the Silver Studio, c. 1902. See cat. 30.

Index

Italic page numbers refer to illustrations.

"Irish Camels," a Donegal showcard dated 1899 and designed by William Findlay, depicts wagon loads of Alexander Morton & Co. rugs headed to market. At least one bundle (at center) appears to be bound for New York. Courtesy V & A Images, Victoria and Albert Museum.